Praise for A TEACHER'S STICK UP FOR YOURSELF!

"*A Teacher's Guide to Stick Up for Yourself!* is as enlightened as it is creative. The authors have created a resource that can be applied in a variety of settings by educators that are new or experienced. In tackling the topics of self-esteem and assertiveness, this text offers users the opportunity to equip young people with tools that will enable them to reach their full potential. The quality of instructional ideas and subject matter found in these pages is sure to keep the book relevant for years to come."

—**Andrew Hawk, M.S.**, special education teacher, Lafayette, Indiana

"Self-advocacy is the greatest skill a student can learn for leadership, relationships, and school. *Stick Up for Yourself!* offers skills to help students reason through expectations, needs, and goal setting, then gives practical ways to use this information in everyday life. The teacher's guide is absolute gold, giving lesson plans that are detailed and perfect for a seasoned educator or anyone new to running groups. My students and I are so lucky to have this resource that I can use as a stand-alone and also incorporate into other groups."

—**Stephanie Filio, M.Ed.**, middle school counselor, Virginia Beach, Virginia

"*A Teacher's Guide to Stick Up for Yourself!* is a great resource for any teacher wanting to help students recognize the importance of self-esteem, increase their personal power, and build inner security. The book presents strategies necessary to explore these ideas in a positive, straightforward, and helpful way, along with great activity ideas, discussion questions, and resources. Together with *Stick Up for Yourself!*, it's a must-have book for teaching kids to be secure and confident."

—**Felicia Murillo**, K–6 gifted specialist and consultant, Clive, Iowa

"This is a wonderful resource. It's very thorough and scripted for groups but also allows for the flexibility to tailor it to your students' needs."

—**Stephanie Meyer**, guidance counselor, Eriksson Elementary School, Canton, Michigan

REVISED & UPDATED 3RD EDITION

A TEACHER'S GUIDE TO STICK UP FOR YOURSELF!

EVERY KID'S GUIDE TO PERSONAL POWER AND POSITIVE SELF-ESTEEM

AN 11-SESSION COURSE IN SELF-ESTEEM AND ASSERTIVENESS FOR KIDS

GERSHEN KAUFMAN, Ph.D., and LEV RAPHAEL, Ph.D.

Text copyright © 2019, 2000 by Gershen Kaufman, Ph.D., and Lev Raphael, Ph.D.
Illustrations copyright © 2019 by Free Spirit Publishing Inc.

All rights reserved under International and Pan-American Copyright Conventions. Unless otherwise noted, no part of this book may be reproduced, stored in a retrieval system, or transmitted in any form or by any means, electronic, mechanical, photocopying, recording, or otherwise, without express written permission of the publisher, except for brief quotations or critical reviews. For more information, go to www.freespirit.com/permissions.

Free Spirit, Free Spirit Publishing, and associated logos are trademarks and/or registered trademarks of Free Spirit Publishing Inc. A complete listing of our logos and trademarks is available at www.freespirit.com.

ISBN-13 978-1-63198-325-2

Free Spirit Publishing does not have control over or assume responsibility for author or third-party websites and their content.

Edited by Alison Behnke
Cover and interior design by Emily Dyer

10 9 8 7 6 5 4 3 2 1
Printed in the United States of America

Free Spirit Publishing Inc.
6325 Sandburg Road, Suite 100
Minneapolis, MN 55427-3674
(612) 338-2068
help4kids@freespirit.com
www.freespirit.com

Free Spirit offers competitive pricing.
Contact edsales@freespirit.com for pricing information on multiple quantity purchases.

CONTENTS

List of Reproducible Pages vii

Introduction 1
    What Is Self-Esteem and Why Should We Teach It? 1
    About This Book 2
    About the Sessions 3
    General Guidelines 4
    Your Role as Teacher 4
    Your Role as Discussion Leader 5
    Child Protection Laws 6
    About the Evaluations 6
    Getting Support for Yourself 7

Getting Ready 8
    Scheduling the Sessions 8
    Time Requirements 8
    Informing and Involving Parents and Caregivers 8
    Preparing Your Space 9
    Group Discussion Guidelines 9
    Relating Activities to Your Group 10
    Using the "Get Personal" Activities 10
    Before the First Session 11

The Sessions 15
    1: What Does It Mean to Stick Up for Yourself? 16
    2: You Are Responsible for Your Behavior and Feelings 22
    3: Making Choices 32
    4: Naming Your Feelings 38
    5: Claiming Your Feelings 48
    6: Naming and Claiming Your Dreams 58
    7: Naming and Claiming Your Needs 68
    8: Getting and Using Power 78
    9: Building Self-Esteem 86
    10: Building Inner Security 96
    11: Sticking Up for Yourself from Now On: Reviewing Your Choices 108

Additional Activities Across the Curriculum 122

Resources 125

About the Authors 127

LIST OF REPRODUCIBLE PAGES

The following pages are available to download. Please see page 127 for instructions on how to access them.

Letter to Parents and Caregivers	12
Session Topics and Reading Assignments	13
Group Discussion Guidelines	21
Questions for Role-Play	30
How to Keep a Happiness List	31
Talk Things Over with Yourself (Talk About Feelings)	56
Talk Things Over with Yourself (Talk About Dreams)	66
How to Keep an I-Did-It List	67
Seven Needs	75
Talk Things Over with Yourself (Talk About Needs)	76
Six Good Things to Do for Yourself	106
Role-Playing Scenarios: Coping with Fear and Worrying	107
Role-Playing Scenarios: Power and Choice with Other People	115
Scripts for Talking Things Over with Yourself	116–117
Student Course Evaluation	118–119
Parent and Caregiver Course Evaluation	120–121

INTRODUCTION

WHAT IS SELF-ESTEEM AND WHY SHOULD WE TEACH IT?

Positive self-esteem is the single most important psychological skill we can develop in order to thrive in society. Having self-esteem means being proud of ourselves and experiencing that pride from within. Without self-esteem, kids doubt themselves, cave in to peer pressure, feel worthless or inferior, and may turn to drugs or alcohol as a crutch. With self-esteem, kids feel secure inside themselves, are more willing to take positive risks, are more likely to take responsibility for their actions, can cope with life's changes and challenges, and are resilient in the face of rejection, disappointment, failure, and defeat.

Self-esteem is *not* conceit, it's *not* arrogance, and it's *not* superiority!

Unfortunately, it's often confused with all three (and also with narcissism, egotism, and disrespect), which leads some people to believe that too much self-esteem is bad for kids. In fact, nothing could be further from the truth. Indiscriminate praise, flattery, social promotion, and falsely inflated self-worth are indeed bad for kids, but those aren't what self-esteem is really about. Self-esteem is based on facts and truths, achievements and competencies. The more self-esteem kids have, and the stronger it is, the better equipped they are to make their way in the world.

Conceit, arrogance, and superiority do exist, of course. But they aren't the result of genuine pride. Instead, they're the result of *contempt* for others. Pride grows out of enjoying ourselves, our accomplishments, our skills, and our abilities. It's not about diminishing anyone else.

Contempt, on the other hand, often masquerades as pride, but it's really false pride if you look closely. When we're contemptuous of others, we perceive them as being beneath us. We see ourselves as superior. Secretly, however, we're actually feeling *inferior* to others. Contempt allows us to temporarily rise above those feelings of inferiority. But in order to keep feeling this way, we have to continually find someone else to feel superior to—someone else we can put down in order to stay on top.

We believe that contempt is a root cause of two great problems facing our schools—and our world—today: bullying and violence. Kids who taunt, tease, and harass others aren't kids with positive self-esteem and genuine pride in themselves. They are kids who lack social skills and empathy, and may have other serious problems, including parents or older siblings who bully them, deep-seated anger, loneliness, jealousy, or resentment of another person's success. In order to bully others, you must believe that their feelings, wants, and needs don't matter. You must feel contempt for them.

When contempt combines with feelings of powerlessness and shame, these emotions can escalate into violence. We've seen this in the school shootings that shock us so profoundly year after year. The children and teens who wound and kill their classmates and teachers aren't kids with positive self-esteem and genuine pride in themselves. For reasons we may never fully understand, these kids developed utter contempt for others, coupled with a burning rage. It wasn't only that other people's feelings, wants, and needs didn't matter. Their *lives* didn't matter.

Self-esteem isn't the culprit here. Rather, the *lack* of positive self-esteem may lead some kids to take inappropriate, hurtful, and even violent or desperate actions. When we help kids build positive self-esteem, we're not teaching them to diminish anyone else, and we're certainly not teaching them to be contemptuous. Instead, we're teaching them to take pride in themselves; to feel good about themselves when they do the right thing and own responsibility when they don't; to celebrate their achievements (both tangible and intangible); to know what they stand for and what they won't stand for; and to strive to be their best inside and out. When kids have a solid grasp of their feelings and needs, trust their emotions and perceptions, have a realistic sense of their capabilities, and have personal power, *then* they feel secure and confident inside themselves and don't feel the need to put down other people.

Self-esteem isn't something we're born with. It's something we learn, which means it can be taught. We believe that all children should be taught the skills of personal power and positive self-esteem at home and in the classroom right along with reading, writing, and arithmetic. All these "basics" work together.

ABOUT THIS BOOK

A Teacher's Guide to Stick Up for Yourself! helps children and young people in fourth through eighth grades build self-esteem, become more self-aware, and develop and practice assertiveness skills. It was designed for the classroom, but it can also be used in other group settings, including counseling groups, after-school programs, youth groups, clubs, and community programs.

It is intended to be used with the student book, *Stick Up for Yourself! Every Kid's Guide to Personal Power and Positive Self-Esteem*. Students are asked to read portions of that book before and/or during each session, so you'll want to have several copies on hand if possible. Ideally, each student will have his or her own copy.

The student book is based on a program originally developed for adults. Called "Affect and Self-Esteem," it was taught as an undergraduate course in the Psychology Department at Michigan State University. That adult program is also available in book form, titled *Dynamics of Power: Fighting Shame and Building Self-Esteem*. To create *Stick Up for Yourself!* we adapted its concepts, principles, and tools specifically for children ages nine to thirteen. By reading the book and doing the "Get Personal" writing exercises, children can learn essential self-esteem concepts on their own. That learning becomes especially powerful in a classroom or group setting, where children benefit from the guidance of a caring adult leader and the opportunity to explore the concepts more fully in activities and discussions.

A Teacher's Guide includes clear and complete instructions for eleven consecutive sessions. Each session is presented in a logically organized, step-by-step way, with the final session being devoted to review and evaluation. The sessions are scripted so you can literally read many parts aloud, if you like. (Within the sessions, this scripted text is in **bold** type.) Our goal was to create a guide that would be welcoming and easy to use for any classroom teacher or adult group leader, beginning or experienced.

A Teacher's Guide also includes suggestions for additional curriculum-related activities and a list of resources.

ABOUT THE SESSIONS

The sessions are:

1. What Does It Mean to Stick Up for Yourself?
2. You Are Responsible for Your Behavior and Feelings
3. Making Choices
4. Naming Your Feelings
5. Claiming Your Feelings
6. Naming and Claiming Your Dreams
7. Naming and Claiming Your Needs
8. Getting and Using Power
9. Building Self-Esteem
10. Building Inner Security
11. Sticking Up for Yourself from Now On: Reviewing Your Choices

Each session includes the following parts:

- An **overview** that introduces and briefly describes the session topic(s).
- A list of **learner outcomes** stating the purpose of the session and what your students should be able to do after participating in the session.

- A list of all the **materials** (handouts, writing materials, and so on) you and your students will need for the session.
- An **agenda** giving you an at-a-glance plan for the entire session.
- A series of **activities and discussion prompts** that guide you step-by-step through the session, from introduction through closing. Each activity relates to one or more of the learner outcomes.

GENERAL GUIDELINES

1. Familiarize yourself with the entire course before you lead the first session. Read this introduction and "Getting Ready" (pages 8–13) first, then read through all eleven sessions and "Additional Activities Across the Curriculum" (pages 122–124). Depending on how much time you have before the course begins, you may also want to consult one or more of the resources listed on pages 125–126.

2. Give yourself time to prepare for each session. Make sure you have all the materials you need, including enough copies of any handouts used in the session.

3. Feel free to make use of the margins in this guide to jot down notes, observations, personal experiences, additional questions, ideas, reactions, and anything else that comes to mind. We hope you'll customize this guide and make it your own.

4. Keep parents, families, caregivers, or guardians informed about what you're doing in the course. Invite their questions before, during, and after. See "Informing and Involving Parents and Caregivers" (pages 8–9).

5. Remember that as a caring, concerned adult, you're in an ideal position to help students build personal power, positive self-esteem, and inner security. Treat them with respect. Encourage them to do their best—without expecting perfection. Allow them to make mistakes and take positive risks. Give them opportunities to make choices and decisions. Invite them to share their feelings, needs, and future dreams. Be someone they trust and can talk to about whatever is important to them.

YOUR ROLE AS TEACHER

In this course, the teaching role may be a little different than what you're used to. You'll structure the activities and organize the physical setting, just as you do in other teaching situations. But the students, in a sense, will determine the content. Their life experiences will form the basis for discussion.

For this reason, you may feel somewhat apprehensive about your ability to respond and to teach. You may not feel the same self-assurance you have in other teaching situations. Two things may help you:

1. being willing to serve as a model for your students
2. being familiar with the tools presented in the sessions

We have found that teachers who are willing to serve as models by sharing their own experiences and feelings are more effective as facilitators of this course. Plus they come away from the course feeling that something significant has happened for everyone, including themselves.

Modeling means letting students see that you, too, have situations in your life that require you to sort through your feelings, figure out which needs are important to meet at the time, and so on. It doesn't necessarily mean you'll be sharing your own story in every activity. But whenever you see an opportunity to help students understand by sharing a personal experience or feeling, we encourage you to do so.

The tools presented in the course include the following: the Happiness List (pages 27–28); the I-Did-It List (pages 63–64); Talking Things Over with Yourself (pages 52, 62–63, and 73); Change Your Inner Voices (pages 91–93); Active Imagination (page 101); and Creating a Personal Shield (page 102). Practice using the tools yourself so you're able to model them for students. If you start writing your own Happiness List and I-Did-It List each day, you'll have examples to share with students when those tools are introduced.

YOUR ROLE AS DISCUSSION LEADER

1. As teacher, you provide the structure. Be clear about the purpose of each session, and let students know that it's your role to keep the session moving along.

2. It's important to try to give everyone who wants to share an opportunity to do so. But sometimes you'll need to move on before a student has said everything he or she wants to. When this happens, say, "I'll come back to you if there's time."

3. Sometimes students will want to share their thoughts and feelings; sometimes they won't. Let them know it's okay to say "I pass." At the same time, encourage students to share whenever they feel comfortable doing so, because sharing allows the group to offer feedback and support. Point out that we also learn a lot by listening.

4. Model support and encouragement when students are talking. Don't judge what they say. Sometimes you may want to point out choices they have in a situation, but never tell them which choice they *should* make or what they

should think. Notice even small ways students are learning and growing, and comment favorably on them.

5. Try not to talk too much; this group is for the students, and you want them to participate. When you have something to say, keep it short and to the point, then bring students back into the discussion.

6. Ask open-ended questions, not those that can be answered with a yes or no. For example, you might ask "How would you feel if . . . ?" rather than "Would you be upset if . . . ?"

7. If you want to bring up a personal experience without identifying it as yours, you can begin by saying "I have a friend who . . ."

8. If someone monopolizes the discussion, gently direct attention away from him or her. You might say "Thank you for sharing. Now let's hear what other group members are thinking."

9. Find ways to involve everyone. If you have a student who isn't ready to participate in discussions, find another role for him or her. Let the student hand out papers or arrange chairs, or ask the student to help you remember to do something.

10. It helps to see life—yours and your students'—as a journey. What you see and hear and learn along the way is amazing. If you can communicate that to students, it may help them accept change as a natural, desirable process.

CHILD PROTECTION LAWS

Confidentiality is important to the success of this course, but there are certain things you may hear or observe that you *must* report for the protection of the child and any others involved.

Before beginning the course, be absolutely sure that you understand exactly what you're legally required to report and what the guidelines for reporting are. These reporting requirements usually fall under the category of child protection legislation.

Most school districts and youth organizations have developed guidelines to conform to child protection laws. Learn what those guidelines are and who you should report to if the need arises.

ABOUT THE EVALUATIONS

It's likely that you'll teach this course more than once, and you'll want to improve each time. Evaluations provide valuable feedback that you can use to strengthen the course and your teaching.

This book includes two formal evaluations: one for students and one for parents, guardians, or caregivers (see pages 118–121). You might use information from completed evaluations to follow up after the course and plan future courses.

Students also have the opportunity to do a self-evaluation. During the first session, they are asked to write about particular situations in which they'd like to learn how to stick up for themselves. During the final session, they are asked to read what they wrote during the first session and decide for themselves if they reached their goals. This helps students integrate their experience and realize what they have accomplished in the course.

The student self-evaluations will also help you, as the teacher, identify which aspects of the course worked best for your students and how you could improve other parts.

GETTING SUPPORT FOR YOURSELF

In a course such as this, where feelings are expressed openly, you can't always anticipate what a session will be like or what needs might be revealed. Things may happen that indicate the need for follow-up, but you might not be sure how to proceed. For example, you may suspect that a child is showing signs of depression but not know if your hunch is accurate. You may notice that one student seems to have a great deal of anxiety. You might wonder, based on what a student shares in the group, if there's a need for counseling or further discussion. You may not know what to do about a student who tends to be disruptive but only in small-group settings. Or you may feel overwhelmed or drained by a particularly emotional session.

Think of someone you can talk to—a school counselor, the school psychologist, a fellow teacher who has led similar classes, or another colleague you trust and respect. Ask if he or she is available to help you debrief after sessions when you feel the need. You can talk about what went on, but you'll want to respect the group's confidentiality, just as you expect your students to do.

For more information about the principles and tools presented in this course, see the resources section beginning on page 125.

GETTING READY

SCHEDULING THE SESSIONS

If possible, schedule the sessions for a time when you can keep outside interruptions to a minimum. For example, try to avoid holding the sessions during a period of the day when class members are regularly called out of the room for various reasons. It's frustrating to get students involved and interested only to be distracted. Especially when feelings are being shared, it's disruptive to have people coming in and out who aren't part of the group and aren't aware of the discussion guidelines.

TIME REQUIREMENTS

Each session is likely to take about 45 to 60 minutes from start to finish. The actual time required will depend on the age of the students as well as the amount of discussion that takes place during the various activities. Sessions 10 and 11 are likely to take more time than the others.

Many sessions also include an optional extension activity; you can use your judgment about whether to include those.

As you teach the course for the first time, keep track of how long each session takes so you'll have that information available when you teach the course again. And if you go on to teach the course to different age groups, also keep track of how the length of time required for the sessions changes as the age of the participants changes.

INFORMING AND INVOLVING PARENTS AND CAREGIVERS

At least one week before conducting the first session, send home a letter to parents, caregivers, or guardians describing the course and telling them when it will start. (*Note:* We use the term *parents* in this book, but your students likely have many different kinds of families, so you can take the word *parents* to indicate whatever adults take care of and are responsible for your students.) A sample letter is found on page 12. You may use this exact letter or use it as a starting point for your own letter. Depending on your situation, you may want to ask parents for their support, and you may need or want to get their written permission for children to take the course.

Encourage parents to read the student book, *Stick Up for Yourself! Every Kid's Guide to Personal Power and Positive Self-Esteem*. Tell students that their parents may ask to borrow the book and suggest that they take it home with them. If parents want to look at the book before the course begins, arrange for them to see a copy.

Invite parents to email, call, or text you (depending on how you prefer to be contacted) with any questions they have before, during, or after the course. Give them your preferred contact information so they know how to reach you, and let them know the best days or times to get in touch if they are calling.

If you're teaching a group that is new to you, you may want to ask parents if there's anything they would like you to know about their children before the program begins.

It's a good idea to stay in touch with parents throughout the course. Consider sending home brief notes about how the course is progressing, or sending parents copies of handouts you use with the students. At the end of the course, invite feedback and comments from parents by sending them the evaluation form on pages 120–121.

PREPARING YOUR SPACE

The physical setting is important to the success of these sessions. If possible, try to organize the room so you and your students can sit in a circle for full-group discussions. Allow space between small groups, but set up the room in a way that also allows you to monitor what's going on in all the groups.

Think about how you might signal the beginning of the session. Turning the lights off and on is one way to get students' attention. You might play a few moments of relaxing music to let them know it's time to begin. Or you may have other ideas. Whatever you choose, you want it to be a pleasant way to help students shift gears.

GROUP DISCUSSION GUIDELINES

You may already have guidelines in place for class or group discussions. If so, make sure that everyone understands them and agrees with them. For the purposes of this course, you'll want your guidelines to include the following:

1. What is said in the group stays in the group.*
2. We are polite and respectful to each other. We don't use put-downs. We want everyone in the group to feel valued and accepted.
3. We listen to each other. When someone is talking, we look at the person and pay attention. We don't spend that time thinking about what we're going to say when it's our turn.

---

* See "Child Protection Laws" on page 6.

4. Everyone is welcome to share their thoughts and feelings, but no one *has* to share. It's okay to say "I pass" if you don't want to share.

5. There are no right or wrong answers.

RELATING ACTIVITIES TO YOUR GROUP

Good teachers are flexible and responsive, and being successful with this course does not necessarily mean teaching it to the letter. As you plan for each session, think about ways you might adapt the activities to your students' needs and relate the examples to their interests. You may decide to modify an activity or example, ask additional questions, or substitute new questions. You may choose to replace or skip some of the activities. As you make changes to the sessions, try to keep the learner outcomes in mind and let them guide your planning.

Many of the activities revolve around students' discussion of their own life experiences. This has the benefit of automatically relating the course to the community in which they live. If students can't relate to an activity, they won't be able to use it as a springboard, and the discussion may fall flat. Often a minor change is all that's needed to help them see connections between the activity and their lives. Take time to read through all the activities for each session before you conduct that session. If you feel that a particular activity isn't especially relevant to your students and their community, modify it so that it *will* speak to your group.

USING THE "GET PERSONAL" ACTIVITIES

The student book includes several writing activities titled "Get Personal." (For examples, see pages 26, 42, and 51 in *Stick Up for Yourself!*) You might use these as optional activities during the course, or assign them when assigning students' reading for each session. Either way, make it clear that students' "Get Personal" writing will remain confidential. Emphasize that they never have to share it with anyone (including you) unless they choose to.

Encourage students to think of the "Get Personal" activities as things they can do now and may want to do again after the course is finished. Point out that their ideas and feelings will be changing along the way, and they may find they have new things to write about.

At a minimum, ask students to read the tips on the bottom half of page 6 in *Stick Up for Yourself!* These briefly explain why the "Get Personal" activities are important and how to make the most of them.

BEFORE THE FIRST SESSION

A week before the course begins:

1. Tell students that next week you'll be starting a new course that will help them build self-esteem and be more assertive. Keep this announcement brief and explain that students will learn more details the following week. Say that they'll need to bring a journal (which could be a notebook or a tablet) to the first session, but that's all the preparation they'll have to do.

2. Send home a letter to parents and caregivers announcing the course. See "Informing and Involving Parents and Caregivers" (pages 8–9). You may want to attach a copy of "Session Topics and Reading Assignments" (page 13) to the letter.

A day or two before the course begins:

1. Remind students about the course's start date, and ask them to be sure to bring their journals to the first session.

2. Make copies of the "Session Topics and Reading Assignments" handout (page 13) and give one to each student (or wait until the first session to do this). You may want to add dates or other information about location and times. If students will be sharing copies of *Stick Up for Yourself! Every Kid's Guide to Personal Power and Positive Self-Esteem*, post a copy of the handout on the reading table or elsewhere in your teaching space.

STICK UP FOR YOURSELF!

Dear Parents and Caregivers,

I'm writing to tell you about an exciting new course called "Stick Up for Yourself!" that the children and I will be starting soon.

This eleven-session course helps kids build self-esteem, become more self-aware, build inner security, and develop and practice assertiveness skills. It teaches them to be responsible for their own behavior and feelings. Through readings, activities, and discussions, kids learn how to make good choices, get to know themselves better, handle strong feelings (like anger and jealousy), cope with worries and uncertainty, and form more positive relationships with the people in their lives (including you).

I want to make it very clear that this course does *not* teach kids to be conceited, arrogant, or disrespectful. That's not what self-esteem is about. Instead, self-esteem is about having the skills and strength to resist negative peer pressure, take positive risks, cope with life's changes and challenges, and feel proud of one's own accomplishments and abilities. We all need self-esteem to survive and thrive—and the earlier we learn it, the better.

You may want to read the book your child will be reading during the course. I encourage you to do so. It's called *Stick Up for Yourself! Every Kid's Guide to Personal Power and Positive Self-Esteem*. Ask your child if you can borrow his or her copy. Or contact me and I'll arrange to loan you a copy.

This course can be a wonderful growing experience for your child. You may notice that he or she is "trying on" new behaviors and ways of relating to you or others. Sometimes new behaviors are awkward; change takes time. You may see a new behavior one day and wonder where it went the next. When this happens, it might help to think about those times in our adult lives when we try to make changes. Changing is often slow for us too.

Please feel free to contact me with any questions you have before, during, or after the course.

Yours sincerely,

Contact information

Email: _____

Text: _____ Phone: _____

Best times to reach me are: _____

The course begins on: _____

P.S. Students want their parents to *know about* the course, but they don't always want to *talk about* it while they're taking it. I suggest you let your child bring it up in discussions with you or your family. Please be patient!

From *A Teacher's Guide to Stick Up for Yourself!* by Gershen Kaufman, Ph.D., and Lev Raphael, Ph.D., copyright © 2019. This page may be reproduced for individual, classroom, or small group work only. For other uses, contact www.freespirit.com/permissions.

Stick Up for Yourself!

SESSION TOPICS AND READING ASSIGNMENTS

All readings are from *Stick Up for Yourself! Every Kid's Guide to Personal Power and Positive Self-Esteem*.

Session	Reading
1. What Does It Mean to Stick Up for Yourself?	pages **1–4** (through "What You Need to Stick Up for Yourself")
2. You Are Responsible for Your Behavior and Feelings	pages **8–14** and pages **87–90** (starting with "How to Live Happily Ever After")
3. Making Choices	pages **15–20**
4. Naming Your Feelings	pages **21–46** (through "Talk About Your Feelings")
5. Claiming Your Feelings	pages **58–71** (starting with "Claim Your Feelings, Future Dreams, and Needs")
6. Naming and Claiming Your Dreams	pages **46–50** (starting with "Name Your Future Dreams"), pages **58–62** (starting with "Claim Your Feelings, Future Dreams, and Needs" and going through "Tips for Talking Things Over with Yourself"), and pages **97–100** (starting with "Keep an I-Did-It List" and going through "Tips for Making the Most of Your I-Did-It List")
7. Naming and Claiming Your Needs	pages **50–62** (through "Tips for Talking Things Over with Yourself")
8. Getting and Using Power	pages **72–87** (up to "How to Live Happily Ever After")
9. Building Self-Esteem	pages **91–97** (up to "Ways to Build Your Self-Esteem"), pages **100–108**, and pages **133–135**
10. Building Inner Security	pages **109–132**
11. Sticking Up for Yourself from Now On: Reviewing Your Choices	no reading assignment

From *A Teacher's Guide to Stick Up for Yourself!* by Gershen Kaufman, Ph.D., and Lev Raphael, Ph.D., copyright © 2019. This page may be reproduced for individual, classroom, or small group work only. For other uses, contact www.freespirit.com/permissions.

THE SESSIONS

SESSION 1: What Does It Mean to Stick Up for Yourself?

Reading Assignment
Stick Up for Yourself! pages 1–4 (through "What You Need to Stick Up for Yourself")

Session 1 introduces the course. Students learn what "stick up for yourself" means. They discover that it doesn't mean getting back at someone else; being bossy, stuck-up, or rude; or saying and doing whatever you want, whenever you want. It means knowing who you are and what you stand for; being true to yourself; knowing how to speak up for yourself, and doing so when it's the right thing to do; and understanding that there's always someone on your side—*you*.

Students are introduced to the idea that the three skills they need to stick up for themselves are personal power, positive self-esteem, and inner security. Throughout the course, they will be learning how to develop these three important skills.

Learner Outcomes
The purpose of this session is to help students:

- prepare for the course
- become familiar with the phrase "stick up for yourself" as it is used in this course
- identify situations in which they feel they need to learn new ways to stick up for themselves

Materials
- *optional:* copies of the "Group Discussion Guidelines" handout (page 21)
- *optional:* copies of the "Session Topics and Reading Assignments" handout (page 13)
- whiteboard, interactive board, chalkboard, or flip chart
- copies of the student book *Stick Up for Yourself!*
- a blank piece of paper for each student
- student journals; have extra notebooks available for students who forget to bring their own

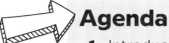

Agenda

1. Introduce students to the course.
2. Ask students to brainstorm what it means to stick up for yourself.
3. Give students time to read pages 1–4 in the student book (through "What You Need to Stick Up for Yourself").
4. Revisit the list students made when brainstorming to see if the reading changed their ideas about what it means to stick up for yourself.
5. Lead the activity "Mix Up," in which situations and ways to stick up for yourself are randomly (and sometimes humorously) matched.
6. Ask students to identify and write down their goals for the course.
7. Close the session and assign the reading for session 2.

ACTIVITY AND DISCUSSION

1. Introduction

Say: **When you're finished with these sessions, you'll have a better understanding of what it means to stick up for yourself. You'll learn about things you can do and say—right now *and* in the future—to stick up for yourself.**

Each time we meet, you'll do some reading and you'll write in your journal. Be sure to have your journal with you at every session.

Before we start, let's make sure we all agree on some basic guidelines.

Review your class discussion guidelines, or hand out copies of "Group Discussion Guidelines" and go over them with the students. *Tip:* During future sessions, you may want to post these guidelines where everyone can see them, to serve as a reminder.

Say: **I encourage you to take part in all the activities and discussions. Sometimes that will mean choosing to share your ideas and thoughts. Other times it may mean just being here and listening. Both are okay.**

During these meetings, we will often spend time listening to each other. It is very important that we all show respect for each other.

If you feel your students need specifics about what it means to be respectful, take a moment to go over those now. *Examples:* Pay attention; don't interrupt; don't sigh or make faces; don't use hurtful words; don't criticize or judge; treat other people as you want them to treat you.

Hand out copies of "Session Topics and Reading Assignments" if you didn't distribute these earlier.

2. What Does "Stick Up for Yourself" Mean?

Ask: **What do you think it means to stick up for yourself?**

As students brainstorm, write their ideas on the board or flip chart, without commenting or asking for clarification.

3. Reading

Ask students to read or review pages 1–4 in *Stick Up for Yourself!* (through "What You Need to Stick Up for Yourself"). Tell them to close their books when they're done so you'll be able to tell they're ready to go on.

4. What Does "Stick Up for Yourself" Mean? (continued)

Go back to the list students brainstormed before reading. Say: **After reading, you may have some new ideas about what it means to stick up for yourself. Let's look at the list we made earlier.**

Now we know that sticking up for yourself doesn't mean getting back at someone else. Is there anything on our list that we might want to change? Anything that might be more about wanting revenge rather than sticking up for ourselves?

Sticking up for yourself doesn't mean acting bossy, stuck-up, or rude. Is there anything on this list we might want to change?

Sticking up for yourself means knowing who you are and what you stand for, and being true to yourself. Are those on our list?

Can you give some examples of things you stand for? What does it mean to be true to yourself?

Speaking up for yourself is one way to stick up for yourself. Is that on our list?

Think about these words: "There's always someone on your side—*you*." What does this mean to you? Should we add this to our list?

5. Mix Up

Give each student a blank piece of paper. Have the group count off by threes (1, 2, 3, 1, 2, 3, and so on) until each member of the class has a number.

Ask the 1s to raise their hands. Say: **Think of the name of a popular actor, singer, or fictional character. Write the name on your paper.**

Ask the 2s to raise their hands. Say: **Think of a situation you might get into at home, at a friend's home, or at school in which you might have to stick up for yourself. Write it on your paper.**

Brainstorm with the 2s for a moment if they need help. Here are some ideas to offer:

- Your older brother borrowed your favorite book without asking.
- Your teacher lost your homework assignment and gave you a zero.
- Your mom forgot to pick you up after football practice.
- The bus driver made you get off the bus because he thought you were shoving and pushing.
- You're playing a game at a friend's home and your friend starts cheating.
- Your friend invites you to work together on an art project for school but then won't let you help.

Ask the 3s to raise their hands. Say: **Think of a way you would stick up for yourself. Write it on your paper.** Show the 3s the list the class made earlier if they need help.

Ask the students to get into groups of 3. Each group should have a 1, a 2, and a 3. Say: **Now we'll go around the room, giving each group a turn. You'll each read what is on your paper. In each group, student number 1 reads the name of the actor, singer, or character. Student number 2 tells us the situation that person or character is in. Student number 3 tells us what the person or character will do. Just read what's on your paper, starting with student number 1, and try to do it fairly quickly. Ready? Let's go.** (If necessary, give students an example to help get them started.)

End the activity by saying: **Sometimes what we do to stick up for ourselves works; sometimes it doesn't.**

Sometimes we have clear ideas about certain ways to stick up for ourselves but aren't aware of other ways. Sometimes we notice how other people stick up for themselves—but sticking up for yourself isn't always something other people can see or hear.

6. Goal Setting

Write on the board or flip chart:

> In these sessions, I want to learn new ways to stick up for myself when . . .

Ask students to take out the journals they brought with them for the course. (Hand out extra notebooks to students who forgot theirs.) Say: **Copy this sentence starter into your journal. Then take a few minutes to finish the sentence. After we've finished all the sessions, you'll look back at what you wrote to see if you learned what you hoped to learn.**

7. Closing

Write on the board or flip chart:

> Personal power (knowing who you are)
>
> Positive self-esteem (liking and respecting yourself)
>
> Inner security (feeling safe and secure inside yourself)

Summarize by saying: **In this session, we started learning what it means to stick up for yourself. These three skills—personal power, positive self-esteem, and inner security—will help you stick up for yourself, wherever you are, whatever situation you are in.**

In the next session, we'll begin talking about personal power. Before the next session, read pages 8 through 14 and 87 through 90 (starting with "How to Live Happily Ever After") in *Stick Up for Yourself!*

If necessary, tell students where and when the next session will be.

STICK UP FOR YOURSELF!

GROUP DISCUSSION GUIDELINES

1. What is said in the group stays in the group.

2. We are polite and respectful to each other. We don't use put-downs. We want everyone in the group to feel valued and accepted.

3. We listen to each other. When someone is talking, we look at the person and pay attention. We don't spend this time thinking about what we're going to say when it's our turn.

4. Everyone is welcome to share their thoughts and feelings. But no one *has* to share. It's okay to say "I pass" if you don't want to share.

5. There are no right or wrong answers.

SESSION 2: YOU ARE RESPONSIBLE FOR YOUR BEHAVIOR AND FEELINGS

Reading Assignment
Stick Up for Yourself! pages 8–14 and 87–90 (starting with "How to Live Happily Ever After")

In **session 2**, personal power is defined as "being secure and confident inside yourself." Personal power is presented as something that everyone can develop. Students learn that personal power has four parts: being responsible, making choices, getting to know yourself, and getting and using power in your relationships and your life.

This session is devoted to the first part: being responsible, specifically for your behavior and feelings. Students learn that even though other people may sometimes do or say things we respond to with a certain feeling or behavior, they didn't *make* us respond that way. Similarly, even though other people respond to what we say or do in a certain way, we didn't *make* them feel or act a specific way. Each of us is responsible for our own behavior and feelings. At the same time, students learn that being responsible isn't the same as being perfect.

One of the main tools used in the course, the Happiness List, is introduced as a powerful way to begin collecting and storing good feelings. This helps us develop personal power and positive self-esteem.

Learner Outcomes
The purpose of this session is to help students:

- identify that being responsible for their feelings and behavior is one way to develop personal power
- identify that anytime they claim "you made me do it" as a way of explaining their feelings and behavior, they are trying to avoid being responsible
- identify that other people's actions or words might trigger a feeling or behavior, but that doesn't mean other people are responsible for that feeling or behavior
- understand that they are responsible for their own feelings and behavior
- discover one new way to stick up for themselves when they make mistakes
- identify the Happiness List as a way to begin collecting and storing good feelings to help them develop personal power

Materials
- an object to represent a wall or barrier, such as a desk, chair, or bookcase
- a sign that says "You Made Me Do It!"
- copies of the "Questions for Role-Play" handout (page 30)
- copies of the student book *Stick Up for Yourself!*
- board or flip chart
- student journals
- copies of the "How to Keep a Happiness List" handout (page 31)

Agenda

1. Introduce the session.
2. Lead the role-play "You Made Me Do It."
3. Give students time to read pages 8–14 and 87–90 (starting with "How to Live Happily Ever After") in the student book if they haven't already done so.
4. Lead a discussion about how other people can trigger our reactions.
5. Lead the activity "Nobody's Perfect" and ask students to write at least one new way they will deal with their mistakes.
6. Introduce and explain the Happiness List. Give students time to write their Happiness Lists for today, and spend time discussing their reactions to this activity.
7. Close the session and assign the reading for session 3.

ACTIVITY AND DISCUSSION

1. Introduction

Say: **Today you'll learn more about how to stick up for yourself. One way to stick up for yourself is by getting and using personal power. Being responsible is an important part of personal power.**

Being responsible doesn't mean carrying the whole world on your shoulders, but it is a big job! In this session, you'll learn about what you are responsible for: *your own* behavior and *your own* feelings.

2. Role-Play: "You Made Me Do It"

Ask: **Has your doctor ever taken a little hammer and tapped it on the front part of your knee? What happened?**

Did you *make* your knee jerk, or did it just happen?

We call this an *automatic response*. When someone does something without thinking, it's sometimes described as a "knee-jerk response." For a few minutes, we're going to talk about words many of us automatically say when something goes wrong and we don't want to be seen as responsible: "You made me do it!"

Those words may be a sign that we're not being responsible for our own behavior and feelings.

Show students an object in the room that suggests a barrier or wall. Place the "You Made Me Do It" sign on it. For example, you could tape a paper "You Made Me Do It" sign to the back of a chair, or you could make the sign out of card stock and set it on top of a desk or bookcase.

Say: **The words "you made me do it" are like a wall we put up. We may do this automatically—like a knee-jerk response—or we may do it only now and then. Either way, whenever we say "You made me do it," it's a sign that we're not being responsible.**

Right now, for fun, you're going to role-play in pairs. One person will ask a question. The other person will answer the question with what we're going to call a "you-made-me-do-it" answer. You won't actually *use* the words "you made me do it," but that's the message you want to get across.

Here's an example. The question is: *"Why didn't you take out the garbage?"* And a "you-made-me-do-it" answer is: *"You didn't put it by the back door, so I didn't know it needed to go out."*

Ask: **Can you think of another "you-made-me-do-it" answer for this question?** If students have trouble thinking of answers, you might suggest one or more of the following:

- You didn't tell me it was full.
- You never said that was my job this week.
- You didn't sort the stuff for recycling.
- You didn't get me up early enough, so I didn't have time.

When you're sure students have grasped the idea, divide them into pairs (or into groups of three or four, if that works better).

Hand out copies of "Questions for Role-Play." Ask students to try to think of at least one "you-made-me-do-it" answer for each question. Tell them they'll only have a few minutes, so they need to work quickly in their pairs or groups. They can skip a question if they have trouble thinking of an answer.

Come back together as a large group for discussion, but have students stay in the physical locations they're in with their small groups. Ask one of the questions. Go from group to group, asking them to quickly give one answer they came up with in their role-plays.

If appropriate, you might say: **It didn't seem that hard for you to come up with answers. I wonder if that means you're experts at this!**

End the activity by saying: **Being responsible for your behavior and feelings can help you get and use personal power.**

At one time or another, you may catch yourself saying to someone, "You made me do it!" But saying "you made me do it" is a way we avoid being responsible. It's a wall we put up that keeps us from getting and using personal power.

Whenever you hear yourself say, "You made me do it," remind yourself: "No one else is responsible for my behavior or feelings. No one made me do it."

3. Reading

Ask students to quickly review pages 8–14 in *Stick Up for Yourself!* Tell them to close their books when they're done so you'll be able to tell they're ready to move on. Then ask: **If someone talks you into doing something, are you responsible for your behavior?**

What if you do something without thinking—you "just do it"? Are you responsible then? Why or why not? When has this happened to you?

If you do something you really didn't *mean* to do, are you responsible? Why or why not? When has this happened to you?

Can someone else *make* you feel angry or sad or happy? Why or why not?

If students have trouble with this last question, remind them of the point by saying: **What other people say or do may *trigger* your feelings, but they didn't *make* you feel that way. You alone are responsible for your own feelings.**

Then say: **Turn to page 13 in *Stick Up for Yourself!* Find what the authors say is the main reason to be responsible. When you find it, raise your hand.**

Ask someone to read aloud what they found:

> The main reason is because it's the best thing to do for you. Being responsible helps you feel secure and confident inside yourself. It gives you a feeling of *personal power*.

Say: **It may take time before you're comfortable with the fact that you're responsible for your own behavior and feelings. Change takes time.**

Changing the way you think about things is like wearing a new pair of shoes. Sometimes it takes a while before new shoes are comfortable to walk in. They may even pinch your feet. But if you keep wearing them, they start to feel more comfortable and natural—like they're a part of you.

Keep in mind that being responsible is a way to get and use personal power.

4. Triggers

Ask: **Have you ever said to someone, "I knew you would say that!" or "I knew you would do that!" Can you give me an example?**

How did you know what the person was going to do or say?

Lead the discussion until someone expresses the idea that we know what people are going to do or say because we've seen them react that way in similar situations. Then ask: **How many of you can think of something that you might say to someone that you feel sure would result in that person crying or getting angry? Why do you feel so sure about that?**

Help students see that we begin to predict people's behavior because (1) we've seen them react in similar situations, and (2) we know what's important to them. Then say: **Even though you're responsible only for your own behavior, sometimes your behavior might trigger a behavior or feeling in another person. Here are two examples:**

- **You didn't *make* your friend cry. But when you didn't ask her to your party, she felt sad. Not getting an invitation was a trigger for her sadness.**

- **Your brother didn't *make* you angry. But when he spilled paint on your new shirt, it was a trigger for your anger.**

Ask: **If your mom always gets angry when you leave dirty dishes in the sink, are you responsible for her feeling angry? Are the dirty dishes a trigger?**

Do you think that leaving dirty dishes in the sink would be a trigger if you had never done this before? Is it more likely to be a trigger if you have done it many times?

Tell everyone to pair up with a person nearby. Then say: **Take turns. First, tell about something you do that triggers a feeling or behavior in someone else. Then tell about something another person does that triggers a reaction in you. First something *you* do; then something *another* person does.**

After two or three minutes, bring the class back together and ask: **Would anyone like to share what they do that triggers a reaction in someone else?**

Did anyone think of something another person does that triggers an angry feeling in you? A hurt feeling? A happy feeling? An excited feeling? A scared feeling? A feeling of shame?

Can you think of one way that being aware of triggers can help you?

5. Nobody's Perfect

Ask: **Has anyone here ever made a mistake? Raise your hand if you've made one mistake.**

Is there anyone who has made two mistakes? Three? More than three? More than you can count?

Who is the Mistake Champion of our group?

If appropriate, you might say: **I'm sure I've made more mistakes than any of you. You haven't lived as long as I have.**

Ask: **Now, is there anyone here who thinks they're never going to make another mistake?**

Who would like to think they're not going to make the *same* mistakes?

Say: **You're going to make mistakes. We all are. It's part of life. Being responsible means you don't blame someone else for your mistakes. You admit your mistakes and learn from them.**

It matters what you tell yourself when you make a mistake. You can help or hurt your self-esteem.

Ask: **What do you tell yourself when you make a mistake?**

Do you know what it means to forgive yourself?

Write on the board or flip chart:

> When I make a mistake, I usually tell myself . . .
>
> From now on, when I make a mistake I'm going to tell myself . . .

Ask students to open their journals. Say: **In your journal, copy the sentences I've written here. Then finish them with your own ideas.**

End the activity by saying: **Every human being has the right to make mistakes every day. That includes you.**

6. The Happiness List

Say: **Turn to a clean page in your journal.** Then ask: **Has anybody ever told you that you're a collector? What did they mean?**

Say: **Some people collect lots of things, and the spaces where they live or work or go to school become filled with these things. We do this with feelings too. We collect feelings. And those collected feelings become part of a bigger and bigger collection.**

It's important to have lots of positive feelings in your collection. Remembering happy, positive feelings is one way you help yourself feel secure and confident, no matter what!

Collecting and storing feelings can help you get and use personal power—*if* your collection is made up of positive feelings.

Pages 87 through 90 in your book talk about the Happiness List. Turn to page 89 and follow along as I read the five reasons it's so important to keep a Happiness List every day:

> 1. It boosts your *personal power*.
> 2. It teaches you that *you are responsible* for your own happiness.
> 3. It teaches you that *you can choose* how to experience your life.
> 4. It teaches you to look for things that *create* happiness.
> 5. It teaches you how to *collect and store* positive feelings.

Say: **Today we're going to start keeping a Happiness List. We'll do this for the rest of these sessions—or maybe for the rest of our lives! Who knows? We could end up with the greatest collection of positive feelings in the history of the world!**

These don't have to be big things. Noticing small things can make us happy too. Start to notice what makes you smile. Those are the things you want to put on your list. Let's get started.

Right now, write down five things that happened today—things you feel good about, that put a smile on your face.

Give students time to write. Then ask: **Was this easy for you to do, or hard? Does anyone want to tell how they felt about doing this?**

Anyone else?

Say: **There are four simple steps you can follow to keep a Happiness List and collect lots of positive feelings.**

Hand out copies of "How to Keep a Happiness List." Read it to students or ask them to read:

> 1. STOP everything and notice what's making you happy.
> 2. FEEL the happy feeling.
> 3. STORE it inside you.
> 4. WRITE it down as soon as you can.

End the activity by saying: **Keep a Happiness List every day. Start your collection and watch it grow!**

In future sessions, we'll talk more about the Happiness List. For now, just get started.

7. Closing

Summarize by saying: **In this session, we learned that we are responsible for our own behavior and feelings. We are *not* responsible for other people's feelings or behavior—only our own.**

One way to be more responsible is to stop saying "you made me do it."

We also learned about triggers. Sometimes our behavior triggers certain feelings or behaviors in other people. But we didn't *make* them feel or act that way. They are responsible for their behavior and feelings, just as we are responsible for our own.

Sometimes other people's behavior triggers certain feelings or reactions in us, but they didn't *make* us feel or act that way. We are responsible for our behavior and feelings, just as they are responsible for their own.

Everyone makes mistakes. It's important to expect to make mistakes every day. It's also important to forgive ourselves when we make mistakes.

One way to get and use personal power is to collect positive feelings. Keeping a Happiness List will help us do that.

In the next session, we'll begin talking about another important part of developing personal power: making choices.

Say: **Before the next session, read pages 15 through 20 in *Stick Up for Yourself!***

If necessary, tell students where and when the next session will be.

STICK UP FOR YOURSELF!

QUESTIONS FOR ROLE-PLAY

Where is your homework?

Why didn't you call like you said you would?

Why did you wear my sweater without asking?

What happened to the change from the $5 I gave you?

Why are you late to class?

Why aren't the dishes washed?

Who broke this?

Tell me why you didn't get the grade you expected on this test.

STICK UP FOR YOURSELF!

HOW TO KEEP A HAPPINESS LIST

Whenever something happens that puts a smile on your face:

1. **STOP** everything and notice what's making you happy.

2. **FEEL** the happy feeling.

3. **STORE** it inside you.

4. **WRITE** it down as soon as you can.

Try to do this five times every day. Weekdays and weekends. School days and holidays. Be happy five times every day.

SESSION 3: MAKING CHOICES

Reading Assignment
Stick Up for Yourself! pages 15–20

Session 3 helps students develop an understanding of the statement, "Because you are responsible for your own behavior and feelings, you can make choices about them."

In this session, students learn the importance of identifying and making choices. Activities help students learn to separate feelings from acting on feelings, and understand that while they have some choices regarding how they feel, they have *more* choices in what to do about the feeling.

The relationship between expectations and feelings is also discussed. To determine what their expectations are, students can learn to ask, "What do I hope will happen? What are the chances it *will* happen?" Having realistic expectations helps students develop personal power.

Learner Outcomes
The purpose of this session is to help students:

- understand that they can choose how to feel
- understand that they can choose what to do about a feeling
- identify realistic and unrealistic expectations
- identify ways in which their feelings and their expectations are sometimes connected

Materials
- copies of the student book *Stick Up for Yourself!*
- board or flip chart
- student journals

Agenda

1. Introduce the session.
2. Give students time to read pages 15–20 in the student book, if they haven't already done so, and have a brief discussion.
3. Lead the activity "Choices." *Optional:* Conclude this activity with a role-play.
4. Lead the activity "What Do You Expect?" to help students identify realistic and unrealistic expectations.
5. Lead the activity "Becoming More Realistic" to develop students' understanding of how expectations influence feelings.
6. Close the session and assign the reading for session 4.

ACTIVITY AND DISCUSSION

1. Introduction

Say: **This session is about choices you can make in how you feel and act. How many of you often say or think, "I didn't have a choice"?**

Sometimes you're right. You don't always have a choice about something you have to do. But sometimes you overlook choices. This session will help you begin to notice the choices you have. Identifying choices and making positive ones are things you can do to stick up for yourself.

2. Reading

Ask students to read or review pages 15–20 in *Stick Up for Yourself!* Tell them to close their books when they're done so you'll be able to tell they're ready to go on. Then say: **In your book, you read about Maria, who got a math test back from her teacher. The teacher had written, "You can do better!" Imagine yourself in that situation for a minute. How would you feel?**

Maria could feel angry or bad about herself. Or she could decide that what she did was good enough. That is a way to stick up for herself.

Who has had an experience like Daniel? When you needed to talk to someone right away, but you couldn't get the person's attention for one reason or another? How did you feel? Why do you think you felt that way? What did you do? What else could you have done?

Being able to identify choices we have about our feelings and our actions gives us personal power.

3. Choices

Say: **We're going to take a few minutes to listen to a story about a boy named Obi. We'll practice identifying possible choices he has.**

Ask the class to listen as you read the following. (You may need to read the story more than once.)

> Obi is at a friend's apartment. His mom wants him to be home by 8 p.m. sharp. That means he needs to catch the 7:30 bus.
>
> Obi stays too long at his friend's place and misses the bus. The next one comes at 8:00—but it won't get him home until 8:30, a half hour late.
>
> He could take the subway at 7:45 and still make it home by 8:00—but his mom has told him never to ride the subway after 7:00.

Stop the story and ask: **What choices does Obi have?**

Allow time for discussion. Students may pick up on the fact that regardless of what Obi decides, he's going to break one of his mom's rules. Either he takes the bus and arrives home late, or he takes the subway when he's not allowed to.

Continue the story:

> Obi tries calling his mom, but there's no answer. He decides to take the bus and be late.

Stop the story and ask: **What do you think of the choice Obi made? Why?**
Continue the story:

> When Obi gets off the bus at his stop, his mom is there waiting for him. She doesn't look happy.

Stop the story and ask: **What choices does Obi have now? In what he feels? In how he acts?**
Continue the story:

> The first thing his mom says is, "You're half an hour late. You're grounded!"

Ask: **What do you think Obi is feeling right now? What choices does he have right now in how he feels or acts?**

What could he say or do that might help the situation? What could he say or do that might make the situation worse?

Note: You may either conclude the activity at this point or do a brief role-play. If you're ending the activity now, say: **We can't always predict what choices we're going to have to make. Sometimes we make good choices, sometimes not so good.**

We gain personal power when we learn to recognize—on the spot—the choices that are ours to make.

> ### Optional **Role-Play**
>
> Ask: **Has anyone here ever come home later than you were supposed to?**
>
> Have the group split up into pairs. In each pair, ask the person whose first name starts with the letter closest to the beginning of the alphabet to play the role of the parent. Ask the other person to play the role of the child.
>
> Say: **Here's the situation: If you're playing the child, you're just walking into your home. You're an hour late, and your parent is waiting for you.**
>
> **Whichever role you are playing, take a couple of minutes to decide two things: (1) how you're going to act, and (2) how you're going to let us know what you're feeling.**
>
> Bring the class back together and ask for volunteers to begin the role-play. Afterward, ask the class: **Did you have any trouble figuring out what each person was feeling? Was there a moment when either person seemed to make a choice?**
>
> Ask for volunteers for one more role-play. Say: **This time, I want you to act out the scene without using words.**
>
> After the role-play, ask the class: **Did you have any trouble figuring out what they were feeling?**
>
> End the activity by saying: **We have choices in how we act and how we feel. We gain personal power when we learn to recognize—on the spot—the choices that are ours to make.**

4. What Do You Expect?

Say: **Sometimes we set ourselves up for disappointment. One way we do this is by hoping something will happen that isn't likely to happen.**

Write on the board or flip chart:

> Recipe for Disappointment:
> We *hope* something will happen that isn't *likely* to happen.

Session 3

When we don't get what we hope for, we may become angry or sad. We might even feel that it's somehow our fault. In this activity, we're going to practice identifying the kinds of things we may hope for that set us up for disappointment.

Give this example: **What if I told myself, "I'm going to smile at you more often, because if I smile, it will make you all feel very happy"?**

What do I expect to happen because I smile? Do you think that is a realistic expectation? Is it likely to happen? *(No, it is not realistic.)*

What if, instead, I told myself, "I'm going to smile at you more often so you'll all be able to see how much I enjoy being with you"? Is that a realistic expectation? Is it likely that my smiling will let you know I like being with you? *(Yes, this is realistic.)*

Choose three of the following sentence starters (or others you feel may be more relevant to your group) and write them on the board or flip chart:

> If I grow two inches taller . . .
>
> If I change my hair style . . .
>
> If I try out for the team . . .
>
> If my writing wins an award . . .
>
> If I get popular with the right group . . .
>
> When I leave home . . .
>
> When I have a boyfriend/girlfriend, my life will be . . .
>
> If I go to a different school next year . . .

Divide the class into groups of two or three. Then say: **Each small group will make up endings for the sentences on the board—but some groups will come up with *realistic* endings, and others will create endings that are *not realistic*.**

Go around to each group and whisper to them whether they are to make up realistic or unrealistic endings.

After a few minutes, bring the groups back together. Read the first sentence starter. Ask one of the small groups to read aloud the ending they wrote. Then ask the rest of the class: **Was that a realistic or unrealistic ending? Why do you think so?**

The unrealistic endings are likely to be obvious. Some of the realistic endings may be debatable, and you'll want to allow some time for discussion. Move on before the discussion begins to drag.

Continue until each group has had at least one chance to contribute. End the activity when it's clear that the class understands the difference between realistic and unrealistic expectations. Then ask: **Who can summarize for us how realistic expectations can influence our feelings?**

5. Becoming More Realistic

Say: **I want you to think of something that happens in your life that you often or always feel angry or sad about. Think about that feeling for a minute.**

Turn to a clean page in your journal. I'm going to read three sentence starters. I want you to finish each sentence, describing the feeling you're thinking about right now.

Read each of the following sentence starters, pausing for a moment after each one to give students time to write:

- I think I feel that way because . . .
- What I always hope will happen is . . .
- The chances it will happen are . . .

Say: **Now I want you to think of something that happens in your life that you often or always feel happy about. Think about that feeling for a minute.**

In your journal, finish those same three sentences again, this time describing the feeling you're thinking about right now. (Read the sentence starters again if necessary.)

Ask: **In the situations you wrote about, is it possible that your feelings had a lot to do with what you hoped or expected would happen? Would anyone like to share your thoughts with us?**

End the activity by saying: **Start being more aware of times when you feel angry or sad. When it happens, ask yourself, "What was I expecting?" This may help you figure out whether you have realistic expectations for yourself and for other people, or unrealistic expectations.**

6. Closing

Summarize by saying: **In this session, you learned that part of sticking up for yourself is making choices, on the spot, about how to feel or act.**

Sometimes you may feel disappointed or angry or sad because your expectations are not realistic. Having realistic expectations can help you develop more personal power.

Say: **Before the next session, read pages 21 through 46 in *Stick Up for Yourself!* (through "Talk About Your Feelings"). The next time we meet, we'll talk about feelings and learn how to give them names. This reading assignment is longer than usual, so please make sure to read it ahead of time.**

If necessary, tell students where and when the next session will be.

SESSION 4: NAMING YOUR FEELINGS

Reading Assignment
Stick Up for Yourself! pages 21–46 (through "Talk About Your Feelings")

In **session 4**, students learn to name their feelings. They discover that one part of getting to know themselves is calling feelings by their correct names. This is an essential session, because students' personal power is dependent on whether they are able to accurately name, and then claim or own, the feelings they are experiencing in any situation. Activities and discussions will teach students that their physical reactions and facial expressions can serve as important guides for identifying their feelings more precisely.

Learner Outcomes
The purpose of this session is to help students:

- understand that part of sticking up for themselves is knowing what they are feeling
- identify and name feelings
- understand that knowing accurate names for feelings makes it easier to communicate precisely what they are feeling

Materials

- copies of the student book *Stick Up for Yourself!*
- slips of paper, each with the name of one low-intensity feeling written on it (see student book page 25)
- *optional:* slips of paper with the names of combined feelings written on them (see student book pages 40–46)
- a mirror
- board or flip chart
- student journals

Agenda

1. Introduce the session.
2. Review one part of the reading assignment and tell how the reading will be used in this session.
3. Review another part of the reading assignment and lead the role-play "Name That Feeling." *Optional:* Expand the readings and role-play to include combined feelings.
4. Lead the discussion "What Your Body Is Telling You" to help students learn to notice how their bodies can help them name their feelings.
5. Lead the activity "Recipe for a Good Feeling" to help students identify "ingredients" that might result in a certain feeling.
6. Close the session and assign the reading for session 5.

ACTIVITY AND DISCUSSION

1. Introduction

Say: **In earlier sessions, we learned two ways to get personal power:**

1. **being responsible for your feelings and behavior**
2. **making choices**

Today we're going to begin talking about a third way to get personal power: getting to know yourself. An important part of knowing yourself is knowing what you're feeling. This session is about naming your feelings.

2. Reading

Have students turn to page 23 in *Stick Up for Yourself!* Tell them to follow along silently while you read aloud the first three full paragraphs on page 23:

> Feelings have their own special names. The more names you know, the more you can understand your feelings and tell other people about them. And the more you can stick up for yourself.
>
> Names are like handles for your feelings. Knowing the right name for a feeling allows you to "pick it up," learn about it, and make choices about it.
>
> Calling feelings by their right names adds to your personal power. Calling feelings by their wrong names takes away from your personal power.

Say: **We're not going to take time right now to read or review all the pages on feelings. Instead, we'll be reading certain sections as we do the activities in this session.**

. . . .

3. Name That Feeling

Ask: **Has anyone ever asked you, "How do you feel about what happened?" and you couldn't think of an answer?**

Before you can tell someone what you're feeling—or even describe it to yourself—it helps to have a name for that feeling.

Turn to page 25. We're going to take a few minutes to talk about the nine low-intensity feelings listed at the bottom of the page.

Let's start with *interest*. I'd like someone to volunteer to read the first paragraph on page 26, which tells about *interest*. Stop when you get to "Things and people . . ."

Follow this procedure until you have gone through all nine feelings on the low-intensity list: *interest, enjoyment, surprise, fear, distress, anger, shame, dissmell, disgust.*

Note: Have students read only the descriptions of the feelings, not the lists of things, times, or events that might trigger those feelings. For some of the readings, you may need to tell students where to start and stop. Here are the readings:

> **INTEREST** (page 26): When you're *interested* in something, you're very curious about it. You concentrate on it because it holds your attention, and you want to learn and know everything you can about that thing or idea. Similarly, when you're interested in a person, you're fascinated by them and what they do, like, or say.
>
> **ENJOYMENT** (page 27): When you're *enjoying* yourself, you're smiling contentedly and feeling very pleased and satisfied. You feel happy and warm all over.
>
> **SURPRISE** (pages 28–29): When you're *surprised* by something, you may not know how to react at first. You weren't expecting what happened, so you're not sure what to do. Maybe you don't say or do anything for a moment or two. You need time to absorb the experience.
>
> **FEAR** (page 30): When you're *fearful*, you're feeling frightened or worried. You think something bad is about to happen, or someone is about to threaten or hurt you. Fear signals that you are in danger, or that you believe you are in danger. A threat may really

exist, or you may only be imagining it. But imagining something dangerous can still *feel* very real.

DISTRESS (page 31): When you're *distressed* about something, you feel sad inside and you feel like crying.

ANGER (page 33): Anger can be sudden and fierce, here in a moment and gone in a flash. Or it can start slowly, gradually build, and then burn for a long time. You might feel *angry* at a particular person or about a particular thing. Or you might feel angry at everyone and everything.

SHAME (page 34): When you feel *shame*, you feel like everyone is looking at you—judging you. It's like they can see inside you. Shame is about feeling worthless and exposed—revealed as ugly inside. It can feel like your protective covering has suddenly been stripped away, allowing others to see you as *lesser*. And although you want desperately to hide, it's as though you're caught in the burning glare of a spotlight. It might feel like nobody could *ever* like you or respect you. Shame is like a wound deep inside you.

DISSMELL (page 37): When you experience dissmell, it's usually because suddenly something or someone close to you smells very bad and you have to pull away quickly. Dissmell is our natural response to bad odors, to anything that's foul-smelling.

DISGUST (page 38): When you're *disgusted* with someone (or something) you can't stand to be around that person or thing. They make you sick to your stomach. You want to be rid of them, the way you would spit out something that tastes awful. At times you might even feel disgusted with yourself.

Say: **Now let's do a role-play. I'm going to divide you into small groups. Each group will get a slip of paper with the name of a feeling written on it. Your group has to figure out how to show us that feeling—without using any words. You can't talk about it; you can only act out the feeling or show that feeling on your face.**

Decide as a group whether everyone in your group will do the exact same thing, or if you'll each do something different. For example, one member of your group could use their posture and body language to act out the feeling assigned to your group, and someone else could show us a facial expression of that same feeling. Remember, you can't tell us the name of the feeling. You have to *show* us.

Session 4   **41**

If you can't figure out what to do, you can reread the part of your book that talks about that feeling.

You can also reread the part of your book that describes each feeling's unique facial expression (beginning on pages 39). You can even look in the mirror we have here in class while you're preparing to act out a feeling to see how it shows on your face. Then you can use this information to show your classmates which feeling you're acting out.

When you're at home, you can also try to look in a mirror whenever you're having a feeling in order to see how that feeling shows on your face.

Any questions? *(Answer any questions they have.)*

You'll need nine groups for this activity, so divide the class into groups of two, three, or four depending on the number of students you have. Give each group a slip of paper with the name of the feeling they are to act out. Allow them some practice time, and then call the groups together. Choose one group to begin.

After the group shows the feeling, ask the others: **What feeling are they acting out? Why do you think so?**

What helped you decide? Was anything confusing?

Continue until each group has had a chance to contribute. End by saying: **In this activity, we practiced naming feelings based on what we saw. Nonverbal behavior helped us "read" and name feelings.**

> **Optional Combined Feelings**
>
> If time allows, expand the readings and role-play to include the combined feelings described on pages 40–46 of the student book. You might start by asking: **Who can tell me what happens when you mix red and blue together?** *(They combine to make purple.)* **What about when you mix blue and yellow?** *(Green.)* **Red and yellow?** *(Orange.)*
>
> **The nine feelings we just learned about are like colors. Sometimes they combine. When they do, they create other feelings. These feelings have names too.**
>
> Read aloud the following descriptions of the four combined feelings discussed in the student book:
>
> > CONTEMPT (page 41): To feel *contemptuous* is to look down on other people. You think you're better than they are. You feel as if there's something wrong with them, and they don't deserve to be liked or respected. Contempt is a combination of *anger* and *dissmell*.

JEALOUSY (pages 42–43): To feel *jealous* is to feel very bad inside because you are being excluded or you think you are. Jealousy involves at least three people, one of whom is you. If you're feeling jealous, you are craving someone's affection or attention. If that person shows affection for or interest in someone else, *you* want to be the focus of that attention. You might suddenly view the person receiving affection as a rival. You may feel less worthy or even inferior—like there's something wrong with *you*. At the same time, you might feel angry and resentful. Jealousy is a combination of *shame* and *anger*.

LONELINESS (page 44): To feel *lonely* is to feel like an outsider. You want to feel close to someone, or you want to belong to a group, but instead you feel shut out, ignored, and unwanted. It seems like no one understands you, wants to be with you, or cares about you. Loneliness is a combination of *shame* and *distress*.

DOWN MOOD (page 45): When your mood is up, you feel excited or joyful. You're smiling and might even be bouncing up and down as you walk. When your mood is *down*, your head hangs low, your shoulders sag, and you might feel like crying. Inside you feel empty or worthless. You might feel like a failure—like you just want to bury your head in a pillow and cry. Just like loneliness, a down mood is a combination of *shame* and *distress*.

Include the combined feelings in the role-play. Depending on the size of your class, you might need to have some small groups act out more than one feeling.

4. What Your Body Is Telling You

Before you begin this activity, write on the board or flip chart the names of the seven high-intensity feelings listed on page 25 of the student book:

Excitement

Joy

> Startle
>
> Terror
>
> Anguish
>
> Rage
>
> Humiliation

Note: Dissmell and disgust are included among the low-intensity feelings listed on page 25 of the student book, but they can also be high-intensity. You may want to include them in this discussion.

Say: **You can learn a lot about your feelings by listening to what your body is telling you.**

Think about the last time you were really angry—so angry you were full of rage. How does it feel to be *enraged*? Where in your body do you feel rage?

Write students' answers beside *rage* on the list. Their answers might include: I clench my fists; my face feels hot; I feel like screaming.

What about *terror*? How does your body help you know you're *terrified*?

Write their answers beside *terror* on the list. Their answers might include: I can't move—I feel like I'm frozen stiff; my stomach feels tight; my face or hands get cold; my body shakes; my knees shake; my teeth chatter; I'm sweating.

What about *startle*? How does your body let you know you're *startled*?

Write their answers beside *startle* on the list. Their answers might include: I yell out loud; I jump back; my shoulders lift or hunch up; my mouth opens and my eyes blink.

Continue until you have written at least one or two bodily or facial reactions beside each of the seven high-intensity feelings on the list.

End the activity by saying: **While you're learning to name your feelings, it helps to tune in to what your body is telling you. You experience feelings not only in your mind but also on your face and in your body.**

With practice, you'll get better at naming your feelings. Knowing what you're feeling can help you know what to do about the feeling.

Imagine using your vocabulary of feelings like a musician uses a tuning fork—but instead of tuning a musical instrument, you're tuning your feelings by sharpening your awareness. You're becoming more aware of yourself by putting feelings together with their names. And you're also connecting how they *feel* on the inside with how they *look* on the outside.

5. Recipe for a Good Feeling

Say: **For fun, let's make up a recipe for a good feeling.**

We know the amounts of each ingredient, but we don't know what the ingredients are. Let's start with *joy*. **Each ingredient has to be something that might bring about that feeling.**

Write the following recipe starter on the board or flip chart:

> JOY
>
> 1 quart of _____
> 1 cup of _____
> 2 tablespoons of _____
> ½ teaspoon of _____
> dash of _____
>
> Bake for _____

Say: **Here's what we know so far.** *(Point to the recipe and read what you have written.)* **Now let's finish the recipe.**

Write students' suggestions on the board next to the ingredients. If students have trouble getting the idea, give this example:

> 1 quart of Saturday afternoon
> 1 cup of good friends
> 2 tablespoons of funny jokes
> ½ teaspoon of snacks
> dash of sunshine
>
> Bake for 2 hours

When the students' recipe is finished, have someone read it aloud. Then say: **Turn to a clean page in your journal and write your own recipe for a feeling you would like to have more often. You might write a recipe for enjoyment or joy, or for interest or excitement.**

If you want, you can look at pages 26 through 29 in *Stick Up for Yourself!* **and find more names for these positive feelings. Look under the "Get Personal" boxes for lists of more names. You may call your feeling any name you want, as long as it feels right and true for you.**

Give students time to write their recipes. Then ask: **Does anyone have a recipe they'd like to share?** Say: **You don't have to read the amounts—just your ingredients. Then we'll see if we can figure out what the feeling is.**

Session 4 **45**

End the activity by saying: **There's more than one recipe for joy (or interest, or excitement, and so on). But if we stop and think about it, we can usually figure out why we feel a certain way. That helps us understand our feeling much better, which adds to our personal power.**

Try to be more aware of your feelings. When you notice a feeling, think about it for a few minutes. Ask yourself, "What's happening around me and inside me right now?" You'll learn more about what makes you feel mad or sad or glad.

6. Closing

Summarize by saying: **In this session, you learned that naming your feelings is an important part of getting to know yourself.**

You learned that one way to name your feelings is to listen to what your body is telling you.

Another way is to look in a mirror to see what your face is showing you. Remember to do this at home when you can.

When you're able to give your feeling the correct name, you can choose what to do about it.

Say: **Before the next session, read pages 58 through 71 in** *Stick Up for Yourself!* **(starting with "Claim Your Feelings, Future Dreams, and Needs"). The next time we meet, we'll talk about what it means to claim feelings, and you'll learn how to do it.**

If necessary, tell students where and when the next session will be.

CLAIMING YOUR FEELINGS

Reading Assignment
Stick Up for Yourself! pages 58–71 (starting with "Claim Your Feelings, Future Dreams, and Needs")

The primary goal of **session 5** is to help students understand what it means to *own* a feeling (claim it as their own). Students learn that once they own a feeling, they can begin to identify choices they have for dealing with it. Talking Things Over with Yourself is introduced as a way to help identify feelings and understand choices. Students also learn ways to step outside of feelings at times when their feelings are too powerful to deal with.

Learner Outcomes
The purpose of this session is to help students:

- understand that part of sticking up for themselves is claiming (owning) their feelings
- understand how using the Talking Things Over with Yourself tool can help them learn more about their feelings
- identify ways to detach from or let go of feelings that are too strong to cope with at the moment
- identify positive ways to deal with strong feelings

Materials

- copies of the student book *Stick Up for Yourself!*
- board or flip chart
- one blank slip of paper for each student, plus a box or bag to put the slips in
- copies of the "Talk Things Over with Yourself (Talk About Feelings)" handout (page 56)
- student journals
- extra copies of the "Session Topics and Reading Assignments" handout (page 13)

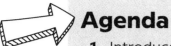

Agenda

1. Introduce the session.
2. Review the reading assignment.
3. Lead the activity "What Does It Mean to Claim a Feeling?" and briefly discuss ways to *avoid* claiming a feeling.
4. Lead the activity "Talking Things Over with Yourself" to help students learn more about a feeling, on the spot, by having a conversation with themselves.
5. Lead the activity "Great Escapes" to help students identify their choices when a feeling is too strong to handle at the moment.
6. Lead the activity "Dealing with Strong Feelings" to help students recognize that there are positive ways to handle strong feelings and adults they can talk to about their feelings.
7. Close the session and assign the reading for session 6.

ACTIVITY AND DISCUSSION

1. Introduction

Say: **In this session, we'll continue talking about feelings. During the last session, you learned to *name* your feelings. This session is about *claiming* your feelings.**

Naming and claiming your feelings helps you get to know yourself and builds your personal power.

2. Reading

Ask students to read or review pages 58–60 in *Stick Up for Yourself!* starting with "Claim Your Feelings, Future Dreams, and Needs." Tell them to raise their hands when they get to "Talk Things Over with Yourself" but to keep their books open. Then ask: **What do the authors say about locking up feelings inside yourself or trying to push them away? Let's find that part and read it again.**

Have students locate the first two paragraphs on page 60. Ask a volunteer to read them aloud:

> You may try to push away some feelings, future dreams, and needs, or lock them up inside yourself. This isn't a good idea, because they don't stay away or hidden. They can turn into problems later.

Session 5 **49**

> Many adults have problems in their lives. Doctors and psychologists think one reason for this is because these adults denied or buried important feelings, future dreams, and needs when they were kids. When we do this, we lose track of who we are. We lose our *selves*.

Say: **In this session, you'll learn about claiming your feelings instead of pushing them away or locking them up inside yourself. Later on, you'll learn about naming and claiming future dreams and needs.**

3. What Does It Mean to Claim a Feeling?

Say: **Let's take a couple minutes to see if we can remember the names of feelings we talked about during the last session. Without looking in your book, can you think of one? Another one? Any more?**

As students name the feelings, list them on the board or flip chart. They may name all the feelings, but if they don't, say: **Now look back at page 25 in your book. Which feelings did we miss?**

Continue until you've listed all the low-intensity and high-intensity feelings on the board or flip chart. Then say: **We also learned the names of four combined feelings. Can anyone remember what they are?** *(Contempt, jealousy, loneliness, and down mood.)*

Add the combined feelings to the list. Then say: **In the last session, we learned that it's important to know the names of feelings. This makes it easier for us to talk about what we're feeling and do something about it.**

It also makes it easier for us to claim our feelings.

Think about how you're feeling right now. What is the name of your feeling? Maybe it's one of the feelings we've listed. Or maybe none of those words describes exactly how you feel.

If you want, take a few moments to look at pages 25 through 46 in *Stick Up for Yourself!* **The authors have listed more names of feelings, plus names for opposites of each of the feelings. Maybe one of those names works better for you.**

Once you have a name for your feeling, come to the front of the room, take a slip of paper out of the box [or bag], and write your feeling's name on the paper. Then take it with you and return to your seat.

Allow time for students to complete this part of the activity. Then say: **Guess what? All of you just claimed your feelings. You thought about how you were feeling. You named your feeling. You wrote it down. Now you** *own* **it. It's** *yours.*

Claiming a feeling isn't that hard. In fact, it's easier than the things people sometimes do to *avoid* **claiming a feeling. Let's talk about some of those things and why they don't work.**

Write on the board or flip chart:

> **WAYS TO AVOID CLAIMING A FEELING**
>
> Push it away.
>
> Lock it up inside yourself.
>
> Question it.
>
> Judge it.
>
> Ignore it.
>
> Call it by a wrong or an inaccurate name.

Lead a brief discussion about each item on this list. Don't dwell too long on any item. The point is to help students see that these are not effective ways to deal with feelings. Start by asking: **What happens when you try to push away a feeling? Is it even possible? Can you push away feeling afraid or angry or jealous? Will the feeling stay away?**

What about when you lock up a feeling inside yourself? In the last session, we talked about how you can learn about your feelings by looking at the expression on your face and listening to what your body is telling you. Do you think it helps or hurts your body if you lock your feelings inside?

What about when you question a feeling? Like, "Hey, anger! What are you doing here?" Is that a good way to do something about the feeling? Why or why not?

Does it help to judge a feeling? What if you decide, "This is a bad feeling," or "This is a good feeling"? Look at page 24 of your book to see what the authors say about this. When you find it, raise your hand.

Have a volunteer read aloud these sentences from page 24 of the student book:

> Feelings aren't wrong or right, bad or good. *Feelings just are.*

Ask: **Is it possible to ignore a feeling? Does that help? Why or why not?**
What happens when we call a feeling by the wrong name instead of by its correct name?

If students don't remember, direct them to page 23 of their book. Have a volunteer read this sentence aloud:

> Calling feelings by their wrong names takes away from your personal power.

Say: **Some of these ideas are a little hard to understand. Even grown-ups have trouble with them sometimes. So here's a fun way to remember them: Imagine that your feeling is a brand-new puppy. It's *your* puppy, nobody else's.**

Ask: **What happens if you try to push it away? Lock it up? Question it? Judge it? Ignore it? Call it by another name—like "kitty" or "goldfish"?**

What's the best way to take care of your new puppy? *(Claim it!)*

End the activity by saying: **When we claim a feeling, we name it and accept it fully. At that moment, it becomes part of us.**

Claiming a feeling doesn't mean we're stuck with it forever. Feelings come and go. Claiming a feeling just means we *know* what we're feeling and we *own* it.

4. Talking Things Over with Yourself

Say: **You can learn a lot about your feelings by talking things over with yourself. Today we're going to practice doing that.**

Hand out copies of "Talk Things Over with Yourself (Talk About Feelings)." Then say: **Before you work on your own, let's look over the script on page 60 in *Stick Up for Yourself!* to get some ideas of how to do this.**

Notice that your "Talk Things Over with Yourself" sheet has the same questions as the script in the book, but there are blanks for you to fill in. Take a few minutes and write about what you're feeling right now, at this moment. Maybe it's the same feeling you claimed a few minutes ago, or maybe it's a different feeling.

You won't have to share your writing with anyone else unless you want to. This is just for you.

You might write about a feeling you'd like to change. Or you might write about a feeling you'd like to keep the way it is. Either is okay, as long as you write about what you're feeling right now.

After a few moments, ask: **What did you learn from doing this?**

Did anyone have trouble figuring out what you were feeling? Does anyone want to share what you found out about your feeling?

Did anyone have trouble figuring out what to do about your feeling? Does anyone want to share what you decided to do about your feeling?

Sometimes you can't change a feeling right away. It takes time. By talking things over with yourself, you may get some ideas about what to do about the feeling or whatever is triggering the feeling.

End the activity by saying: **Keep this script in your journal. It will help you remember the questions to ask when you want to talk feelings over with yourself.**

5. Great Escapes

Say: **We've all had feelings that were so strong we didn't know what to do. After we claim a feeling, we may decide we want to leave it behind for now because it seems too strong to deal with at the moment.**

On pages 62 through 64 of *Stick Up for Yourself!*, **the authors talk about four Great Escapes. Turn to page 62 so we can quickly review what they are. Who can tell me what one of the four is? Another? A third? The fourth?**

Someone here may already use one of these escapes. Ask: **Does anyone use laughing as an escape? What do you find to laugh about?**

Does anyone use exercise—like swimming or biking or dancing—to turn your attention away from a feeling and focus your attention outward onto what you're seeing, hearing, and touching? How well does it work for you? In what type of situations do you use it?

Say: **Sometimes we're in situations where we can't, right then, take a walk or find something to laugh about. It helps to have a way to escape a feeling, even when you can't physically escape the scene. Let's learn a way right now.**

Is there anyone in this room who has blown bubbles using a wand and bubble soap? Then you know how much fun it is to blow a really *big* **bubble and watch it float away.**

That's the idea behind the relaxation tool we're about to practice. Take a feeling you need to be away from, put it inside a bubble, and let it float away.

Even if you don't have a feeling right now that you want to escape, you might have something that's worrying you. We all have something we worry about, even if it's just now and then. You can use this tool to get away from a worry.

Lead students through the following relaxation exercise:

1. Sit comfortably in your chair with your feet flat on the floor. If you feel comfortable doing so, close your eyes.
2. Take a few deep breaths. Breathe in through your nose, and breathe out through your mouth.
3. Breathe in, breathe out. Breathe in, breathe out. Feel yourself relax.
4. Think for a minute about something that has been bothering you lately—it might be anything, big or small.
5. Picture yourself holding a huge bubble wand and a bottle of bubble soap. The bubble wand is as tall as you are, and the soap bottle takes up the whole corner of this room.
6. See yourself dipping the wand into the bottle.

7. Blow into the wand now. Watch a huge bubble start to form.

8. As the bubble forms, imagine your feeling or worry going into the bubble. *(Pause for 10 to 15 seconds.)*

9. Watch the bubble float away, taking your feeling or worry with it. *(Pause.)*

10. Let it go. *(Pause.)*

11. Blow another bubble. Put another feeling or worry inside. *(Pause.)*

12. Watch it float away. *(Pause.)*

13. Let it go. *(Pause.)*

(Wait a few moments, then say:)

14. Now take a deep breath, in through your nose, out through your mouth.

15. Feel what it's like to have your feeling or worry gone for now. Open your eyes again if you've closed them.

Conclude the relaxation exercise by saying: **Different people have different ways of letting go of feelings. The next time you have a feeling that's too strong to deal with at that moment, think about one way you can escape from it or let it go until it becomes more manageable. Then come back to it later and talk it over with yourself.**

6. Dealing with Strong Feelings

Say: Taking a Great Escape isn't the same as pushing away a feeling, ignoring it, or any of the other things we talked about earlier. It's a way to take good care of yourself until you're ready to handle the feeling.

Sooner or later, though, you *will* have to deal with your feeling. Especially if it's a strong feeling—like fear, distress, anger, shame, jealousy, loneliness, or a down mood.

You might not be able to change a strong feeling right away. That takes time. But you don't have to let it control your life.

Pages 65 through 71 of *Stick Up for Yourself!* give you lots of ideas for handling strong feelings. Those pages were part of the reading assignment for today's session.

If you didn't read them yet, try to read them soon. You may want to read them more than once. Or, if you have one of the strong feelings named in the book, read that section first. You might even want to copy some of the ideas into your journal.

You'll notice that every section ends with the same idea: *Talk with an adult you trust.*

Say: **Turn to a clean page in your journal. Write the name of an adult you trust and can talk to. This might be a parent or guardian, an aunt or uncle, a grandparent, a grown-up brother or sister, a teacher, a school counselor, a coach, an adult leader of a club you belong to, a neighbor, a religious or spiritual leader, or someone else.**

After you write one name, write another, then another. Try to write the names of *three adults* **you trust and can talk to. Remember them the next time you need help dealing with a strong feeling.**

7. Closing

Summarize by saying: **In this session, you learned that claiming your feelings is an important part of getting to know yourself.**

You learned to talk things over with yourself and figure out what to do about a feeling.

When a feeling is too strong to handle, you learned to let it go for a while. We talked about some Great Escapes you can use to let go of strong feelings until you're ready to deal with them.

You named at least one adult you trust and can talk to.

Say: **Before the next session, read pages 46 through 50 in** *Stick Up for Yourself!* **(starting with "Name Your Future Dreams"). Reread pages 58 through 62 (starting with "Claim Your Feelings, Future Dreams, and Needs" and going through "Tips for Talking Things Over with Yourself"). Also read pages 97 through 100 (starting with "Keep an I-Did-It List" and going through "Tips for Making the Most of Your I-Did-It List").**

These pages are listed on the "Session Topics and Reading Assignments" handout you received at the beginning of the course. If anyone needs an extra copy, raise your hand and I'll give you one.

The next time we meet, we'll be talking about what it means to name and claim your dreams.

If necessary, tell students where and when the next session will be.

STICK UP FOR YOURSELF!

TALK THINGS OVER WITH YOURSELF
(TALK ABOUT FEELINGS)

Ask yourself, "How am I feeling today?" Then name a feeling you're having. Next, talk it over with yourself. Your talk might go like this:

SAY:
I'm feeling _____ today.

ASK:
Why am I feeling _____?

What's happened that I feel _____ about?

SAY:
I'm feeling _____

because _____

ASK:
What can I do about my _____ feeling?

SAY:
I can _____
_____
_____
_____

From *A Teacher's Guide to Stick Up for Yourself!* by Gershen Kaufman, Ph.D., and Lev Raphael, Ph.D., copyright © 2019. This page may be reproduced for individual, classroom, or small group work only. For other uses, contact www.freespirit.com/permissions.

SESSION 6: NAMING AND CLAIMING YOUR DREAMS

Reading Assignment
Stick Up for Yourself! pages 46–50 (starting with "Name Your Future Dreams"), 58–62 (starting with "Claim Your Feelings, Future Dreams, and Needs" and going through "Tips for Talking Things Over with Yourself"), and 97–100 (starting with "Keep an I-Did-It List" and going through "Tips for Making the Most of Your I-Did-It List")

In **session 6**, students learn another way to get personal power: by naming and claiming their future dreams. The main concept presented here is that dreams are personal goals. Dreams are important in developing personal power and positive self-esteem. Two kinds of dreams are discussed: near-future dreams and far-future dreams. Students learn how the two are related. They practice talking a dream over with themselves.

Learner Outcomes
The purpose of this session is to help students:

- understand that part of sticking up for yourself is naming and claiming dreams
- understand how talking things over with themselves can help them learn more about their dreams
- distinguish between near-future and far-future dreams
- identify the I-Did-It List as a way to build positive self-esteem

Materials

- copies of the student book *Stick Up for Yourself!*
- board or flip chart
- student journals
- volleyball
- masking tape
- copies of the "Talk Things Over with Yourself (Talk About Dreams)" handout (page 66)
- extra copies of the "How to Keep a Happiness List" handout (page 31)
- copies of the "How to Keep an I-Did-It List" handout (page 67)
- extra copies of the "Session Topics and Reading Assignments" handout (page 13)

Agenda

1. Introduce the session.
2. Review the reading assignment.
3. Lead the activity "Naming Your Dreams."
4. Lead the game "Dream Volley" to help students practice relating near-future and far-future dreams.
5. Lead the activity "Talking Things Over with Yourself" to help students learn to make choices about their dreams by having a conversation with themselves.
6. Lead the activity "The I-Did-It List."
7. Close the session and assign the reading for session 7.

ACTIVITY AND DISCUSSION

1. Introduction

Say: **In this session, we'll talk about naming and claiming your dreams, which is a way to get to know yourself. It's also a way to get personal power.**

2. Reading

Ask students to read or review pages 46–50 in *Stick Up for Yourself!* (starting with "Name Your Future Dreams"). Tell them to close their books when they're done so you'll be able to tell they're ready to go on. Then ask: **Who can tell me why we need future dreams?**

Give students a chance to answer the question. Then ask a volunteer to read the first paragraph under "Name Your Future Dreams" on pages 46–47 of the student book:

> Your future dreams are your personal goals—the reasons you do what you do. They give your life direction, purpose, and meaning. They guide your decisions and help you define the kind of person you are and who you want to be.

Ask: **Who can tell me how it affects us if we *don't* have future dreams?**

Give students a chance to answer the question. Then ask a volunteer to read the third paragraph under "Name Your Future Dreams" on page 47 of the student book:

> What happens if you don't have future dreams? Then you have no personal goals to give your life direction, purpose, and meaning. You have nothing to guide your decisions and help you define the kind of person you are, the person you want to be. You're like a car without a steering wheel or a ship without a rudder. Future dreams are essential!

Conclude the activity by saying: **In this session, you'll practice naming and claiming your dreams.**

3. Naming Your Dreams

Say: **There are two kinds of dreams for you to think about: dreams for the *near future* and dreams for the *far future*. You need both kinds.**

Let's figure out first what we mean by *near future* and *far future* so we're talking about the same thing. What do you think the *near future* is?

Discuss until you reach consensus. Then ask: **What do you think the *far future* means? When you have finished your education or job training? When you're thirty or forty years old?**

Discuss until you reach consensus. Say: **I'd like to hear about some of your dreams for the far future. I'll tell you some of mine too.**

Write a list of dreams on the board or flip chart as students volunteer. Include some of your own. Say: **Now let's hear some of your dreams for the near future. I'll tell you some of mine too.**

Write a list of dreams on the board or flip chart as students volunteer; include some of your own. Ask: **Which list do you think has the "bigger dreams"—the far-future list or the near-future list? Does that make sense? Why or why not?**

Do you think our dreams for the far future and the near future need to be related? Why or why not?

Say: **In your journal, as quickly as you can, write down ten dreams you have. Don't think right now about whether they are for the far future or near future.**

You won't be asked to share these unless you want to. They are just for you to know about.

Allow time for writing. Then say: **Now, for each dream on your list, decide whether it's a near-future or far-future dream. Put an *N* beside each near-future dream and an *F* beside each far-future dream.**

Did you have both kinds of dreams on your list?

Read one of your far-future dreams to yourself. Do you have a near-future dream to help make your far-future dream come true?

Who has an example you'd be willing to share?

End the activity by saying: **In this activity, we practiced naming our dreams. We learned that there are two kinds of dreams, far-future and near-future. We need both kinds.**

4. Dream Volley

Say: **It's not always easy to come up with near-future dreams related to our far-future dreams. We can imagine ourselves doing or being something in the future, but we're not sure how to get there.**

Let's get ideas from each other. We'll do this by playing a game called "Dream Volley."

Clear an area of the room and position two teams as if they are on opposite sides of a net. Each team will have three rows—a front, middle, and back row. The number of columns students line up in on each side of the "net" will depend on the size of your class. Indicate the net with a line of masking tape on the floor.

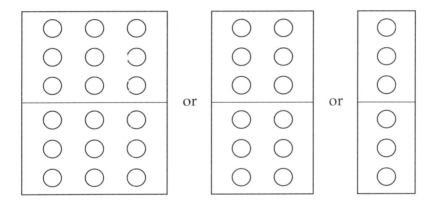

Say: **"Dream Volley" has some rules you have to learn, so listen carefully while I explain them. Then you'll have a chance to ask questions.**

Point out the net (the masking tape). Then explain the rules:

> Rule #1: In this game, you'll gently *toss* the ball to someone on the other side of the net, not hit it over the net.
>
> Rule #2: Before tossing the ball, you'll name a *far-future* dream—something you'd like to do or be someday.
>
> Rule #3: When you catch the ball, you'll name a *near-future* dream related to the far-future dream of the person who tossed you the ball. So be sure to pay attention to two things: who tossed the ball and what that person named as a far-future dream.

> Rule #4: After you name a near-future dream, name a far-future dream of your own. Then toss the ball to someone else and listen to what that person says. He or she might have a good idea for a near-future dream for you.

Ask: **Does everyone understand what we'll be doing? Any questions?**

Answer students' questions. If necessary, say: **Remember: You'll name *two* dreams. First is a near-future dream related to the other person's far-future dream. Next is a far-future dream of your own. When you toss the ball to someone else, that person will name a near-future dream that might help you reach your far-future dream.**

Let's practice before we start. I'll choose two volunteers to demonstrate.

Have one student name a far-future dream. (*Example:* "I want to get a job working with animals.") Then have that student toss the ball across the net to a second student. The second student names a near-future dream related to the first student's far-future dream.

If the second student has trouble doing this, offer a suggestion or two. (*Examples:* "Read books about people who work with animals." "Talk to someone who works at an animal shelter." "Learn about animals by adopting and caring for two hamsters.")

Then the second student names a far-future dream and tosses the ball back across the net to someone else. The student who catches the ball this time names a near-future dream related to the second student's far-future dream.

When the students seem ready, start the game. Allow them to play for five to ten minutes, depending on their interest level and the time you have available. Every so often, you might want to interject a positive comment or two—like "Good idea!" or "Great dream!"

Afterward, have students return to their seats. Say: **We just heard a lot of ideas that can help us reach our dreams. Maybe there's an idea you'll want to try soon.**

End the activity by saying: **It's important to have dreams. Dreams give your life direction, purpose, and meaning. It's also important to have near-future dreams that will help you reach your far-future dreams.**

5. Talking Things Over with Yourself

Say: **You can learn a lot about your dreams by talking things over with yourself. Today we're going to practice doing that.**

Hand out copies of "Talk Things Over with Yourself (Talk About Dreams)." Then say: **Before you work on your own, let's look over the script on pages 60 and 61 in *Stick Up for Yourself!* to get some ideas of how to do this.**

Notice that your "Talk Things Over with Yourself" sheet has the same questions as the script in the book, but there are blanks for you to fill in.

Take a few minutes and write about a dream you have right now for the near future or far future. You won't have to share your dream with anyone else unless you want to. This is just for you.

After a few moments, ask: **What did you learn from doing this?**

Did anyone have trouble figuring out what you have to learn to make your dream happen? By talking things over with yourself, you may get some ideas about what you need to learn.

Does anyone want to share your dream and tell us what you decided to do to help make your dream come true?

Allow time for students who want to share. Then end the activity by saying: **If you want, you can create a plan to start learning and doing things that will help make your dream happen. Write your plan in your journal. You might plan to do one thing tomorrow, another thing next week, another thing by the end of the year, and so on. Whenever you learn or do something related to your dream, write it in your journal.**

Keep this script in your journal to help you remember the questions to ask when you want to talk dreams over with yourself.

6. The I-Did-It List

Say: **In the second session, you learned how to keep a Happiness List to collect and store good feelings. Raise your hand if you've been keeping your Happiness List every day.**

If all students raise their hands, congratulate them and move on. If some don't raise their hands, ask them to reread pages 87–90 of *Stick Up for Yourself!* when they get home (or later today, if there's time) and start keeping their lists. Hand out extra copies of "How to Keep a Happiness List" to students who want or need them.

Say: **Today you're going to begin keeping an I-Did-It List. It's like the Happiness List, but also a bit different. Instead of writing down *things that happen* that put a smile on your face, you write down *things you do* that make you feel proud of yourself.**

These might be activities you take part in. Problems you solve. Successes you achieve. Positive risks you take. Decisions you make. Challenges you meet. Goals you reach. People you help. Accomplishments of any kind. And anything else you feel satisfied with, good about, and proud of.

Like the Happiness List, the I-Did-It List boosts your personal power. It teaches you that you are responsible for feeling proud of yourself. You can choose to do things that make you feel proud. You can look for things to do that create a feeling of pride. You can collect and store proud feelings.

Turn to a clean page in your journal. Right now, write down five things you did yesterday that you feel proud of. These don't have to be big things. Often you do good things when you're just being yourself.

Give students time to write. Then ask: **Did anyone get stuck trying to make a list? Maybe you were trying to think of huge successes. Remember that little things count too. Whatever makes you feel proud can go on your list.**

There are four simple steps you can follow to keep an I-Did-It List and collect lots of proud feelings.

Hand out copies of "How to Keep an I-Did-It List." Read it to the students or ask them to read:

> 1. STOP everything and notice what's making you proud.
> 2. FEEL the proud feeling.
> 3. STORE it inside you.
> 4. WRITE it down as soon as you can.

Say: **Your list could include things like this:**

- **I took out the garbage without being told.**
- **I fed the cat.**
- **I studied for my math test.**
- **I remembered to ask my teacher about makeup work for the day I missed.**
- **I said hi to a new kid at school.**
- **I helped my little sister set the table for dinner.**
- **I tried out for the softball team.**
- **I joined the math club.**

End the activity by saying: **Keeping an I-Did-It List helps you stick up for yourself—with yourself. It helps you gain personal power and build positive self-esteem from inside.**

Being proud of yourself doesn't mean being stuck-up, conceited, or feeling that you're better than other people. It just means enjoying your own accomplishments, skills, and abilities.

Think of your I-Did-It List as a self-esteem savings account. It reminds you of how valuable and worthwhile you are.

Keep an I-Did-It List every day. Also continue keeping your Happiness List. You'll find that it doesn't take much time to keep both lists—and it's really worth it.

7. Closing

Summarize by saying: **In this session, you learned that naming and claiming your dreams is an important part of getting to know yourself.**

You learned that you need to have two kinds of dreams: *near-future* **dreams and** *far-future* **dreams. Your near-future dreams can help your far-future dreams come true.**

You practiced the Talking Things Over with Yourself tool as a way to figure out how to claim your dreams and identify ways to make your dreams come true.

You also learned about the I-Did-It List, which is like a self-esteem savings account.

Say: **Before the next session, read pages 50 through 62 (through "Tips for Talking Things Over with Yourself") in** *Stick Up for Yourself!* **You've already read pages 58 through 62 (through "Tips for Talking Things Over with Yourself"), but please look at them again.**

These pages are listed on the "Session Topics and Reading Assignments" handout you received at the beginning of the course. If anyone needs an extra copy, let me know.

The next time we meet, we'll be talking about what it means to name and claim your needs.

If necessary, tell students where and when the next session will be.

Session 6   **65**

STICK UP FOR YOURSELF!

TALK THINGS OVER WITH YOURSELF
(TALK ABOUT DREAMS)

Ask yourself, "What are my future dreams?" Then name a dream for the near future or far future. Next, talk it over with yourself. Your talk might go like this:

SAY:
I want to _____ someday.

ASK:
What do I have to learn to make this dream happen?

SAY:
I can start by _____
_____
_____

ASK:
What else can I do?

SAY:
I can _____
_____
_____

From *A Teacher's Guide to Stick Up for Yourself!* by Gershen Kaufman, Ph.D., and Lev Raphael, Ph.D., copyright © 2019. This page may be reproduced for individual, classroom, or small group work only. For other uses, contact www.freespirit.com/permissions.

STICK UP FOR YOURSELF!

How to Keep an I-Did-It List

Whenever something happens that makes you feel proud:

1. **STOP** everything and notice what's making you proud.

2. **FEEL** the proud feeling.

3. **STORE** it inside you.

4. **WRITE** it down as soon as you can.

Try to do this five times every day. Weekdays and weekends. School days and holidays. Be proud of yourself five times every day.

From *A Teacher's Guide to Stick Up for Yourself!* by Gershen Kaufman, Ph.D., and Lev Raphael, Ph.D., copyright © 2019. This page may be reproduced for individual, classroom, or small group work only. For other uses, contact www.freespirit.com/permissions.

SESSION 7
NAMING AND CLAIMING YOUR NEEDS

Reading Assignment
Stick Up for Yourself! pages 50–62 (through "Tips for Talking Things Over with Yourself")

Session 7 helps students learn to name and claim their needs. Seven basic needs are presented: relationships with other people; touching and holding; feeling *one* with others and knowing that we belong; being different and separate from others; nurturing other people; feeling worthwhile, valued, and admired; and having power in our relationships and our lives.

Students learn that the more they know about their needs, the more they can understand them and tell other people about them. Knowing their needs and thinking of ways they can be met are important ways to stick up for themselves. Students learn that their needs guide their decisions and help them define what kind of people they are or want to become. They learn how their needs play a role in choosing and building relationships.

Learner Outcomes
The purpose of this session is to help students:

- understand that part of sticking up for yourself is naming and claiming needs
- identify seven needs that are common to all people
- understand how talking things over with themselves can help them learn more about their needs

Materials
- copies of the student book *Stick Up for Yourself!*
- copies of the "Seven Needs" handout (page 75)
- materials for creating a mural (see below)

  Before the session begins, tape the following to a wall somewhere in your space:

  › a large oblong piece of white paper or poster board with "Picture Your Need" written across the top

  Before the session begins, place the following on a table near the paper or poster board:

  › old magazines, catalogs, and/or newspapers with pictures

> drawing paper and colored construction paper
> crayons, colored markers, and colored pencils
> scissors, tape, and glue
- copies of the "Talk Things Over with Yourself (Talk About Needs)" handout (page 76)

Agenda

1. Introduce the session.
2. Review the reading assignment.
3. Lead the discussion "What Do You Need?"
4. Lead the art activity "Picture Your Need" to help students learn to identify how their needs relate to what they do in their daily lives.
5. Lead the activity "Talking Things Over with Yourself" to help students learn to identify their needs by having a conversation with themselves.
6. Review the reasons for keeping an I-Did-It List.
7. Close the session and assign the reading for session 8.

ACTIVITY AND DISCUSSION

1. Introduction

Say: **In this session, we'll talk about naming and claiming your needs, which is a way to get to know yourself. It's also a way to build personal power.**

All human beings have the same basic needs. When our needs are met, we're healthier, happier people.

Sometimes it's difficult to get certain needs met right now. In this session, we'll learn what we might be able to do even when we can't get our needs met.

2. Reading

Ask students to quickly review pages 50–62 (through "Tips for Talking Things Over with Yourself") in *Stick Up for Yourself!* Tell them to raise their hands when they're done but to keep their books open. Then ask: **What do we sometimes really mean when we say we** *need* **something? Like "I need a new computer game" or "I need a haircut"?** *(It really means that we* want *something.)*

Session 7 **69**

Is needing other people a sign we are strong or a sign we are weak? Find a sentence or two in your book that supports your answer.

Have a volunteer read aloud these sentences from page 51 of the student book:

> If you need other people, if you have meaningful and vital relationships with them, then you aren't weak. *You're strong.* Needing and caring for others is a source of strength.

Ask: **Why is it sometimes hard for people to get enough touching and holding in our society? Find that part in your book and listen while I read it.**

Read aloud the following paragraph from page 52:

> Unfortunately, people sometimes confuse touching and holding with sex. That's why, as you get older, you may get mixed messages about touching and holding. Friends who touch each other are often teased. Parents may suddenly start to feel that their kids are too grown-up to be hugged. But this is a problem with how other people think. It isn't a problem with you. It's still okay to need touching and holding—now and for the rest of your life.

Remind students that they need to be very clear about the difference between *good touch* and *bad touch*. Say: *Good touch* **feels good and right. Your mom hugs you. Your friends pat you on the back when you score a basket. Your dad holds you and comforts you when you're feeling sad.**

Bad touch **is when someone—usually a grown-up or an older child—touches you in a way that feels bad or wrong, or in a way you don't want. That person might also tell you to keep it a secret and never tell anyone else about what happened. If that ever happens to you, it's *very* important to say NO! and get away as fast as you can. Then tell an adult you trust. You can also talk to an adult if you're ever confused about** *good touch* **and** *bad touch*.

Earlier, in the session about claiming your feelings (session 5), you wrote in your notebook the names of adults you trust and can talk to about strong feelings. You can also talk to these people about good touch and bad touch.

Ask: **Can anyone tell me what it means to feel** *one* **with other people?** *(We want to be like them, look like them, and act like them—we may even copy their actions and mannerisms. We feel we have things in common with them. We feel close to them; we care about them and they care about us. We learn from them and they learn from us.)*

Why do you think we need to feel *one* **with other people and to belong?** *(This helps us know we're not alone.)*

Say: **At the same time that we need to belong, we also need to be different and separate. Each of us needs to be our own unique self. We go back and forth between these two needs.**

We also need to nurture other people. It makes them feel good, and it makes us feel good inside.

Ask: **Can anyone tell me a time when someone nurtured you, or when you nurtured someone else?**

Say: **We all need to feel worthwhile, valued, and admired. If other people aren't helping us feel worthwhile, valued, and admired, who can do that for us?** *(We can value and admire ourselves.)*

We need to feel we have power in our relationships and in our lives. We'll talk more about this need in the next session.

3. What Do You Need?

Distribute copies of the "Seven Needs" handout. Read it to the students, or ask volunteers to read each sentence in turn:

> 1. The need for relationships with other people
> 2. The need for touching and holding
> 3. The need to feel *one* with others and to belong
> 4. The need to be different and separate from others
> 5. The need to nurture (to care for and help other people)
> 6. The need to feel worthwhile, valued, and admired
> 7. The need for power in our relationships and our lives

Ask: **If you need something, but you don't know what it is, how can you figure out what you need?** *(If a student suggests talking it over with yourself, agree and say you'll be practicing that later in the session.)*

Do you think our feelings or future dreams might give us clues about our needs?

Say: **If I'm feeling lonely, what need might I have?** *(The need for relationships with other people; the need for touching and holding; the need to feel one with others and to belong.)*

If you dream of being in charge of your life and making all your decisions without getting permission from anyone else, what need might this be? *(The need for power in our relationships and our lives.)*

Ask students to come up with other feelings or future dreams and relate them to needs. If they have trouble doing this, you might offer one or more examples:

- I don't like hanging out with my friends right now. I want to spend more time on my own. What might I need? *(To be different and separate from others.)*
- I'm having trouble seeing that anything I do really matters. What might I need? *(To feel worthwhile, valued, and admired.)*
- I wish I were little again so I could curl up in my dad's lap and listen to a story. What might I need? *(To be touched and held.)*

End the activity by saying: **So far, we have practiced naming our needs. We have learned that our feelings and future dreams can give us clues about our needs.**

4. Picture Your Need

Call students' attention to the large piece of white paper or poster board with "Picture Your Need" written across the top. Then say: **We're going to make a mural about needs.**

Each of you will find or draw a picture that relates to one of the seven basic needs. You'll find magazines and art supplies on the table. When you have your picture, tape or glue it to the mural. Don't tell anyone which need it relates to. Keep that a secret for now.

You might bring along your "Seven Needs" sheet to remind you of what the needs are.

When you've put your picture on the mural, return to your seat. Remember, your picture should relate to one of the seven basic needs.

You'll have ten minutes to work on the mural, so let's get started.

Stop this part of the activity after ten minutes, even if some students are still working. When all students are back in their seats, say: **We're going to take a few minutes to see if we can guess the need that each of these pictures represents.**

Point to each picture in turn and ask volunteers to guess which need it relates to. After one or two guesses, ask the student who put the picture on the mural to raise his or her hand. Then ask that person: **What need did you have in mind?**

Note: Take only about half a minute or so for each answer. Stop this part of the activity after five minutes.

End the activity by saying: **We're getting practice thinking about the basic needs and how they relate to our lives. Everyone has the same seven needs. It's important to know about them so we can try to get our needs met.**

5. Talking Things Over with Yourself

Say: **You can learn a lot about your needs by talking things over with yourself. Today we're going to practice doing that.**

Hand out copies of "Talk Things Over with Yourself (Talk About Needs)." Then say: **Before you work on your own, let's look over the script on page 61 in** *Stick Up for Yourself!* **to get some ideas of how to do this.**

Notice that your "Talk Things Over with Yourself" sheet has questions like the script in the book, but there are blanks for you to fill in.

Take a few minutes and write about a need you have right now. You won't have to share your writing with anyone else unless you want to. This is just for you.

After a few moments, ask: **What did you learn from doing this? Did anyone have trouble figuring out how to help yourself meet your need? By talking things over with yourself, you may get some ideas.**

Does anyone want to share your need and tell us one thing you decided to do about it?

Allow time for students who want to share to do so. Then end the activity by saying: **Keep this script in your journal to help you remember the questions to ask when you want to talk needs over with yourself.**

6. The I-Did-It List (Review)

Say: **In the last session, you learned about the I-Did-It List, and I asked you to start keeping the list every day, just like you do with the Happiness List.**

How is it going? Are you finding things to put on your list—things you feel satisfied with and good about? Are you able to be proud of yourself five times every day?

Did anyone get stuck trying to make your list? Were you trying to find huge successes to write about? Remember that little things count too. Whatever makes you feel proud can go on your list.

Simply remembering to make your I-Did-It List is something to be proud of, and can go on your list!

It may take a while for you to notice your successes. We sometimes train ourselves to notice the things we *don't* **do well. That gets in the way of noticing our successes. Just keep writing each day. Make it a habit, and soon it will get easier.**

Remember that your I-Did-It List is like a self-esteem savings account. Don't let it become empty. It reminds you how valuable and worthwhile you are. And that's one of the seven basic needs!

7. Closing

Summarize by saying: **In this session, you learned that naming and claiming your needs is an important part of getting to know yourself.**

You learned that everyone has seven basic needs, and you learned what they are.

You practiced talking needs over with yourself as a way to figure out what you're needing in a situation and how to get a need met.

You also heard a reminder about how important it is to keep writing your I-Did-It List.

Say: **Before the next session, read pages 72 through 87 in** *Stick Up for Yourself!* **(up to "How to Live Happily Ever After").**

The next time we meet, we'll be talking about what it means to get and use power in your relationships and in your life. We'll learn the difference between *personal power* **and** *role power.*

If necessary, tell students where and when the next session will be.

> ### Optional Before the Next Session
>
> Session 8 includes an optional "Power Tune" activity. If you plan to do the activity, say: **We'll also listen to some songs about personal power. If you know a song you think says something about personal power, please bring in a recording of that song a day or two before the next session.**
>
> **Remember that personal power means being** *secure and confident inside yourself.* **It's about being responsible, making choices, and getting to know yourself. When you're looking for a song to bring in, remember what personal power really means.**
>
> Preview songs before the next session. Make sure the lyrics are compatible with your program's standards. For example, you'll want to avoid songs with lyrics that are sexist, racist, homophobic, sexually graphic, or violent.

SEVEN NEEDS

1. The need for relationships with other people

2. The need for touching and holding

3. The need to feel *one* with others and to belong

4. The need to be different and separate from others

5. The need to nurture (to care for and help other people)

6. The need to feel worthwhile, valued, and admired

7. The need for power in our relationships and our lives

STICK UP FOR YOURSELF!

TALK THINGS OVER WITH YOURSELF
(TALK ABOUT NEEDS)

Ask yourself, "Is there anything I need right now?" Try to name your need. Then talk it over with yourself. Your talk might go something like this:

SAY:
I need _____

ASK:
How can I start to get my need met?

SAY:
I can _____
_____
_____

ASK:
What if that doesn't work?

SAY:
I can _____
_____
_____

From *A Teacher's Guide to Stick Up for Yourself!* by Gershen Kaufman, Ph.D., and Lev Raphael, Ph.D., copyright © 2019. This page may be reproduced for individual, classroom, or small group work only. For other uses, contact www.freespirit.com/permissions.

SESSION 8: GETTING AND USING POWER

Reading Assignment
Stick Up for Yourself! pages 72–87 (up to "How to Live Happily Ever After")

In **session 8**, students learn the difference between role power and personal power. Role power is something they have because of what they do (their role). Personal power is something they have because of who they are. Personal power is the most important kind of power they will ever have. It means they can have power over their own lives, even if they never have much role power.

Through discussion, students learn to identify choices they have in situations where they feel powerless. Identifying choices is presented as a way they can realize they do have power in their lives.

Learner Outcomes
The purpose of this session is to help students:

- understand the differences between role power and personal power
- understand that their feelings help them recognize whether people are using power over them in a positive or negative way
- understand that their feelings help them recognize whether they are using power over others in a positive or negative way
- understand that when they are given choices, they feel powerful instead of powerless
- identify choices they can give themselves

Materials
- copies of the student book *Stick Up for Yourself!*
- board or flip chart
- student journals
- *optional:* CD player or other way to play songs brought in by students

Agenda

1. Introduce the session.
2. Review the reading assignment.
3. Lead the activity "Role Power" to help students identify people in their lives who have role power over them. *Optional:* Lead the activity "Power Tune."
4. Lead the activity "Balance of Power" to help students identify ways to develop equal power in a relationship. *Optional:* Expand this activity to broaden the discussion.
5. Review the Happiness List and the I-Did-It List.
6. Close the session and assign the reading for session 9.

ACTIVITY AND DISCUSSION

1. Introduction

Say: **You may remember that personal power has four parts. We've already talked about three of those parts: being responsible for your feelings and behavior, making choices, and getting to know yourself. In this session, we're going to talk about the fourth part: getting and using power in your relationships and your life.**

This session will help you identify ways you already have power in your life, as well as new ways to use your personal power.

2. Reading

Ask students to read or review pages 72–87 in *Stick Up for Yourself!* Tell them to raise their hands when they're done but to keep their books open. Then ask: **What are the two kinds of power?** *(Personal power and role power.)*

As you ask the following questions, record students' answers on the board or flip chart. Ask: **Who can tell me one difference between role power and personal power? What's another difference? Are there any more differences? Any more?**

Students should mention the four differences described on page 74:

- **Role power is something you have just because you're in a certain role.** Personal power means being secure and confident inside yourself.

- **Role power depends on having someone else to be powerful over. (A president without people to govern doesn't have much role power.)** Personal power depends only on you.

- **Role power is something you might have to wait for. You might never have very much role power.** Personal power is something you can have if you work for it. And you can have as much personal power as you want.

- **Only some people can have role power.** Anyone can have personal power. *You* can have personal power even if many people have role power over you.

Ask: **Why is it a waste of energy to fight back against people who have role power over you?** *(It probably won't do any good; it might get you in trouble. You have to accept that there will always be people with role power over you.)*

What can you do with your energy instead of fighting back?

End the activity by saying: **In this reading, you learned there are two kinds of power. Personal power is the most important kind of power you'll ever have. It means you can have power over your life even if you never have much role power.**

. . . .

3. Role Power

Say: **Role power is power you have not because of *who you are*, but just because of *what you do*—in other words, your *role*.**

Right now, there are people in your life who have role power over you. This is true for all of us.

Talk briefly about people who have role power over you in your own life—and why they have role power. Then say: **Turn to a clean page in your journal. Divide it into two columns by drawing a line down the center.** *(If necessary, show students how to do this on the board or flip chart.)*

Write "Role power over me" at the top of the column on the left, and "How I feel about it" at the top of the column on the right. *(Demonstrate if needed.)*

Role power over me	How I feel about it

80 A TEACHER'S GUIDE TO STICK UP FOR YOURSELF!

In the left column, list people who have role power over you right now in your daily life. You can write the person's name or the person's role—like parent, math teacher, coach, and so on.

In the right column, write a word or two that describes how you feel about each person's role power over you. You won't have to share your feelings unless you want to.

You might suggest some words students could use: Okay, So-So, Crummy, No Problem, Super. Or they could use plus or minus symbols, or happy/neutral/sad faces. (You might draw these on the board or flip chart. A happy face has a smile; a neutral face has a straight-line mouth; a sad face has a frown.)

Give students a few minutes to work on their lists. Then ask: **Do you feel the same about all the people who have role power over you?**

Why do you think it feels okay when some people use role power over you and not okay when others do? *(Your goal here is for students to discover that it depends partly on what they ask you to do and how they treat you.)*

Say: **Choose one person on your list. Think about these questions: If you could switch roles and have role power over that person, what would you do the same way he or she does? What would you do differently?**

Who would like to share your thoughts?

If you picture yourself in that person's role, does it make a difference? Does it change how you feel? Is it easier now to accept that he or she has role power over you?

End the activity by saying: **When you accept that some people have role power over you, you can use your energy to build more personal power.**

> **Optional Power Tune**
>
> Depending on how much time is available, play one or more of the songs that students brought in (or an excerpt). After each song, ask: **What words in the song do you remember? What do you think this song says about personal power?**
>
> End the activity by saying: **People talk about power in many ways. Songs are one way. Art is another way. Advertising is a third way. Start noticing images or stories of power. When you see or hear one, think about whether it's about personal power or role power.**

4. Balance of Power

Note: Talking about power in relationships can raise surprising, difficult, or threatening feelings—including feelings about how students perceive their teachers (like you) using role power over them. Be aware of your own feelings, and take time later to be sure you have paid enough attention to what you were experiencing. See "Getting Support for Yourself" (page 7).

Ask: **If you wanted to give a friend power over you, how would you do it?** *(Possible answers: always do what they want to do, always say what they want to hear.)*

Say: **Sometimes we give friends power over us, and we don't even know we're doing it. Our feelings can help us become aware of times when we're giving away our power or times when we're using power over other people.**

We're going to divide into five small groups. In your group, you'll be talking about a time when you felt you *didn't* have equal power with someone else. It may even be a time when you felt totally powerless.

After dividing the class into small groups, point to each group and say:

Group 1, you'll be talking about situations with a *friend*.

Group 2, you'll be talking about situations with your *peer group*.

Group 3, you'll be talking about situations with a *sibling*—a brother or sister. *(Make sure all members of this group have siblings. If they don't, exchange members with another group.)*

Group 4, you'll be talking about situations with a *teacher*.

Group 5, you'll be talking about situations with a *parent or another adult who takes care of you*.

Say: **Each of you will give one example of a situation where you *don't* feel you have equal power, or you feel powerless. Tell the group how you feel when you don't have power. Then ask them for ideas about how you could get more power or equal power. Their job is to come up with choices for you—as many realistic choices as they can.**

Write on the board or flip chart:

1. Give example
2. Say how you feel
3. Ask for ideas or choices
4. Listen

Keep your conversation moving so everyone in your group has a chance to give an example and get ideas for choices.

After a few minutes, bring the groups back together. Say: **I need one volunteer from Group 1 to describe a situation that was discussed and tell what the group suggested.** If necessary, guide students not to reveal what anyone else in their group shared, but to only speak about situations from their own lives.

When the volunteer has finished, ask the class: **How many of you have been in this kind of situation? Does anyone have any other ideas or choices to offer—ways the person in this situation could get more power or equal power?**

Continue until you have heard at least one person from each group.

Note: Since the reading assignment for this session includes a section on "How to Deal with Bullying," it's possible that one or more groups might describe a bullying situation. If this happens, make time for a brief discussion about bullying. You might review the facts about bullying on pages 82–84 of the student book, and the suggestions on pages 84–85.

End the activity by saying: **In this activity, we talked about ways to overcome feeling powerless and ways to develop equal power. It's important to focus on what *you* have power over and the choices *you* can make, instead of trying to change other people.**

> **Optional Power Talks**
>
> Instead of having each group talk about power in only one context—such as with a friend, sibling, or peer group—you may want to schedule another session or sessions so each group can talk about power in all contexts. This would give students a greater opportunity to explore ways to develop equal power in all their relationships.

5. The Happiness List and I-Did-It List (Review)

Ask: **How are you doing with your Happiness List and I-Did-It List?**

Share some of the positive things you've been noticing since you began keeping your own lists. Then ask: **Are you finding things to put on your Happiness List—things that made you smile? Is it getting to be a habit to notice things that make you happy?**

Is it getting easier to identify five things you did each day that you feel proud of?

Remind students of the four steps for keeping each list:

> 1. STOP everything and notice what's making you happy or proud.
> 2. FEEL the happy or proud feeling.
> 3. STORE it inside you.
> 4. WRITE it down as soon as you can.

Say: **The important thing is to keep writing your lists every day. Soon it will become a habit.**

The Happiness List is your collection of positive, happy feelings. Keep collecting.

Your I-Did-It List reminds you how valuable and worthwhile you are. When your self-esteem is strong, you'll feel your personal power.

6. Closing

Summarize by saying: **In this session, you learned that there are two kinds of power:** *personal power* **and** *role power*.

You talked with each other about ways to develop more power or equal power in your relationships.

You learned that having choices gives you more personal power.

Say: **Before the next session, read pages 91 through 97 in** *Stick Up for Yourself!* **(up to "Ways to Build Your Self-Esteem"). Also read pages 100 through 108, as well as chapter 7 ("You Can Stick Up for Yourself") on pages 133 through 135.**

The next time we meet, we'll be talking about ways to build your self-esteem.

If necessary, tell students where and when the next session will be.

SESSION 9: BUILDING SELF-ESTEEM

Reading Assignment
Stick Up for Yourself! pages 91–97 (up to "Ways to Build Your Self-Esteem"), pages 100–108, and pages 133–135

In **session 9**, students learn what self-esteem really means and practice ways to build positive self-esteem. They begin to understand and identify how their inner voices (what they are thinking, feeling, or imagining about themselves) influence their self-esteem. They learn that sometimes their inner voices have a powerful impact on how they feel about themselves. They learn to become more aware of those inner voices and practice ways to change them, so the messages they are continuously sending themselves *about* themselves are positive and self-affirming.

Learner Outcomes
The purpose of this session is to help students:

- understand that they need positive self-esteem in order to stick up for themselves
- identify good things about themselves
- understand what self-esteem really means
- understand how to change critical, blaming, and comparing inner voices into self-affirming inner voices

Materials
- copies of the student book *Stick Up for Yourself!*
- student journals
- slips of paper and a box or bag to put them in
- board or flip chart
- sheets of paper

Agenda

1. Introduce the session.
2. Review the reading assignment.
3. Introduce "Listening to Your Inner Voices" on pages 92–95 in *Stick Up for Yourself!* and have students work with this self-esteem tool.
4. Lead the activity "Change Your Inner Voices: Time to Talk Back" to help students learn how to change negative, critical inner voices into self-affirming inner voices.
5. Have students write role-play scenarios focusing on "Coping with Fear and Worrying" to be used in the next session.
6. Close the session and assign the reading for session 10.

ACTIVITY AND DISCUSSION

1. Introduction

Say: **In this session, we'll focus on positive self-esteem. In order to stick up for yourself, you need to feel good about yourself—to feel valuable and worthwhile.**

We'll practice some tools that will help you build positive self-esteem.

2. Reading

Ask a volunteer to read aloud page 91 and the first paragraph on page 92 of *Stick Up for Yourself!* Then say: **Turn to a clean page in your journal. Quickly write five good things about yourself that you would tell Mr. Hernandez.**

Allow a moment or two for students to do the writing. Then ask: **Who would like to share one or two things you wrote?**

Comment positively on what students say about themselves. ("I'm glad to know that," "I didn't know that about you," "That's terrific," "That's something to be proud of.")

Say: **If you've been keeping your I-Did-It List, you all know lots more than five good things about yourselves. Your self-esteem savings account is growing every day.**

Before we start learning more ways to build self-esteem, there's something important you need to know.

Read aloud the following from page 95 of the student book:

> You might have heard people talk about self-esteem as if it's a bad thing. They think self-esteem means bragging, being stuck-up, and believing you're better than everyone else.
>
> They're mistaken.
>
> Self-esteem means being proud of yourself and feeling that pride on the inside. Not just because you've told yourself, "I'm special and wonderful." Not just because other people have said, "You're special and wonderful." Words alone don't create pride. Actions create pride. Self-esteem means being proud of yourself because you've done things to be proud of.

Say: **No one can *give* you self-esteem. No one can take it away. It's not about anyone else. It's only about *you*.**

3. Listening to Your Inner Voices

Say: **We're going to take the next few minutes to listen to your inner voices and see what they say to you—and about you.**

Turn to a clean page in your journal. Number down the left side from one to ten. I'm going to read ten questions aloud. Each question describes a different situation. You choose the answer—*a* or *b*—that sounds *most like* the way you think or talk to yourself in that kind of situation.

Of course, the answers won't be *exactly* what you'd say. Don't worry about that. Focus on how the answers *feel*. Which one feels most like you, *a* or *b*? Write the letter of your answer in your journal.

Also, try not to answer the way you think you *should* answer. Answer the way you really *would* answer. You won't have to share your answers. No one will know them but you. The goal of this tool is to help you discover how you treat yourself and behave toward yourself on a daily basis.

Read the questions and answers:

> 1. When you get up in the morning and look at yourself in the mirror, what do you say?
>
>   a. "I look great this morning! And I'm going to have a great day."
>
>   b. "Oh, no, not me again! I'm so ugly! Why did I bother to get out of bed?"

2. When you fail at something or make a mistake, what do you tell yourself?

   a. "Everyone has the right to fail or make mistakes every day. Including me."

   b. "I blew it again! I can't do anything right! I should have known better."

3. When you achieve something, what do you say to yourself?

   a. "I'm proud of myself."

   b. "I could have done even better if I had tried harder. It wasn't good enough."

4. You've just talked with someone who has role power over you. (Like a parent, a teacher, or a coach.) What do you tell yourself?

   a. "I handled that pretty well."

   b. "I can't believe I acted so stupid! I always say dumb things."

5. You've just left the first meeting of a new club you joined. What do you say to yourself?

   a. "That was fun. I met some people I liked. They even laughed at the joke I told."

   b. "I talked too much, and nobody liked me. Everyone hated my joke."

6. You've just left a classmate's home after playing together. What do you tell yourself?

   a. "That was fun. We really like each other!"

   b. "That person was just pretending to like me. I probably won't get invited back ever again."

7. When someone gives you a compliment, what do you say to yourself?

   a. "That's nice, and it makes me feel good. Besides, I deserve it!"

   b. "Nobody gives you a compliment unless they want something back. Besides, I don't deserve it."

8. When someone you care about lets you down, what do you tell yourself?

   a. "My feelings are hurt, but I'll get over it. Later, I can try to find out what happened."

   b. "This proves that person doesn't care about me."

9. When you let down someone you care about, what do you say to yourself?

   a. "It isn't nice, and it isn't fun, but sometimes people let each other down. I'll admit what I did, say I'm sorry, hope the person will forgive me, and get on with my life."

   b. How could I do such a terrible thing? I'm so ashamed. No wonder nobody likes me."

10. When you feel needy or unsure of yourself, what do you tell yourself?

    a. "Everyone feels this way sometimes. I'll ask my dad for a hug or curl up with my teddy bear, and I'll feel better soon."

    b. "Why can't I grow up and stop being a baby? What's wrong with me?"

Say: **Now count how many (a) answers you have. Multiply the total by ten.**

Count the number of (b) answers you have and multiply by five.

Add the two scores together. Look at the scoring key on page 95 of your book to find out what your score can tell you about your self-esteem.

You don't need to share your score with anyone. It's for your own information.

Ask: **How many of you agree with your Self-Esteem Rating?**

Say: **If your score is low, don't worry. You're already practicing one important way to build your self-esteem—the I-Did-It List. You'll learn more ways today. But first, let's look at some of the answers one more time.**

If your book isn't already open to page 92, where "Listening to Your Inner Voices" begins, please open it now.

Sometimes we blame or criticize ourselves. If we do this a lot, it lowers our self-esteem. Some of the answers you see in this section are examples of how we might blame or criticize ourselves.

Read the answers until you find an example of blaming. What did you find?

Now find an example of criticizing. What is it?

Can you find another blaming or criticizing answer?

If students have trouble with this, suggest that they read the (b) answers. Then say: **Think for a minute about yourself. Do you blame or criticize yourself? A little bit? A lot? Now and then? You don't need to tell us your answer. Just think about it.**

Sometimes we compare ourselves to other people. When we do, we often end up feeling that we don't measure up—that other people are smarter, or better looking, or they run faster, or they have more friends.

If we spend a lot of time comparing ourselves to others, we may decide we aren't valuable or worthwhile unless we're better than someone else. Can you find an answer that's an example of comparing?

If students can't find one, suggest that they look at (b) in question 5.

Ask: **Do you ever compare yourself to other people? Do you do it a lot? Again, just think about it; you don't have to answer out loud.**

End the activity by saying: **Blaming, criticizing, and comparing are three shaming inner voices we sometimes hear. Those voices hurt our self-esteem.**

But we don't have to listen. We can talk back!

4. Change Your Inner Voices: Time to Talk Back

Ask: **What do you think an "inner voice" is?** *(You want students to say that it's the way we talk to ourselves—including the things we tell ourselves about ourselves. It's how we treat ourselves and how we behave toward ourselves, in ways that produce either positive or negative feelings. If you'd like, you can also define and discuss the term* self-talk.*)*

Say: **If your inner voice is blaming, critical, or comparing, you can change it. There are three important steps for doing this.**

Write on the board or flip chart:

> 1. By saying new, positive, self-affirming words to yourself.
> 2. By experiencing new feelings of kindness and respect for yourself.
> 3. By hearing a new inner voice inside—one that's like the voice of someone you admire. It's the voice of someone who cares about you, encourages you, and respects you—the voice of someone who shows you he or she is proud of you.

Ask: **Can you think of one thing you sometimes tell yourself that's blaming or critical?**

Hand out the slips of paper. Say: **Write one thing you say to yourself when you're being critical of yourself or mean to yourself. You don't have to sign your name. When you're done, come up and put your slip of paper in the box [or bag].**

Take a few moments to silently read through the slips. Then say: **We tell ourselves a lot of shaming things, don't we? I do it too. One thing I catch myself saying is, " _____, you are so _____."** *(Fill in the blanks with your name and something you say to yourself—impatient, stubborn, forgetful, clumsy, and so on.)*

Say: **I'm going to write on the board five of the things you mentioned. Don't worry; no one will know who wrote them.**

Write five student comments on the board or flip chart. Then say: **We can teach ourselves to change those shaming inner voices. Let's practice.**

First, let's think about new words to say. If you say something like this to yourself (point to a student comment), **what new words could you say instead?**

Guide students to come up with positive, self-affirming alternatives to all five of the self-shaming comments. (You might need to give an example or two to get them started.)

Then say: **Next, let's think about new feelings. What have you been doing lately that might help you remember and experience happy or proud feelings?** (Keeping a Happiness List and an I-Did-It List.)

These feelings and memories can help you change inner voices that are shaming, critical, or unkind. Instead of "You're so _____," you can tell yourself, "Remember when you _____?"

Fill in the first blank with one of the student comments from the board or flip chart. Fill in the second blank with a positive comment related to the student comment. You'll have to make this up, since you won't know what students are writing in their Happiness Lists and I-Did-It Lists. For examples, see page 101 of the student book.

Say: **To combine new words and new feelings about yourself you could stop saying things like "You never do anything right." Instead, you can say to yourself "I'm good enough just the way I am."**

Say: **Finally, imagine a new inner voice inside you that is just like the voice of someone you admire—someone who cares about you no matter what happens, who encourages you when you're feeling down, and who shows you respect at all times—even when you fail or make mistakes. Picture this person speaking to you. Be sure to choose someone you like, and who likes you too. This is someone you admire who also admires you, someone who is kind to you and whose voice comforts you.**

If you don't know anyone like this, you can invent someone in your mind.

Say: **Next, imagine the sound of this person's voice. If this person heard you say** (fill in with one of your students' comments) **to yourself, what kind and supportive things would he or she say to you instead?**

Say: **Now say those new, kind words to yourself. Imagine this person is actually speaking the words. Hear this person's voice inside your mind.** *Feel* **what it's like to hear those words.**

Would anyone like to tell us who you're thinking about right now? Whose voice are you hearing? What is that voice saying to you?

End the activity by saying: **The next time you hear a shaming inner voice, remember the three steps for changing it into a positive, self-affirming inner voice:**

1. **Saying new words to yourself.**

2. Experiencing new feelings about yourself.
3. Hearing a new, compassionate voice speaking to you.

These three actions are essential to learning how to build positive self-esteem.

5. Writing Role-Play Scenarios About Coping with Fear and Worrying

Note: If you don't have time for this writing activity but you still want to do the role-playing in session 10, you can use the ready-made ideas in the handout "Role-Playing Scenarios: Coping with Fear and Worrying" (page 107).

Hand out sheets of paper. Say: **We've been learning new ways to cope with strong feelings, like fear, terror, and worry. In the assigned reading for our next session, you'll find out more about how to handle feelings like these.**

During our next session, you're going to role-play ways to handle fear and worrying, using your own role-play ideas.

Now, write about something that's happening in your life—a situation involving something you're either scared about, fearful of, or worry about a lot. Don't sign your name. Just describe the situation.

If students have trouble thinking of something to write, give examples, ranging from relatively common worries to more serious fears:

- I have to play the piano in a recital, and I'm scared that I'll mess up.
- I worry about my family having enough money.
- My dog is really old and I'm worried he might die soon.
- My parents fight sometimes, and I'm afraid they might get a divorce.
- I'm scared about standing up to bullying.
- I'm scared of a hurricane hitting my hometown.
- I worry about shootings at schools, mosques, churches, or synagogues.
- I worry a lot about climate change.
- I'm terrified of a terrorist attacking people.
- I don't always feel safe in my home, school, or neighborhood.

Give students time to write, then collect their papers. End the activity by saying: **During our next session, we'll role-play as many of these as we have time for. This will give you new tools to counteract fear and reduce worrying.**

6. Closing

Summarize by saying: **In this session, you learned ways to build and improve your self-esteem.**

First by *listening* to your inner voices, which reveals how you treat yourself. Next by *changing* your inner voices, which strengthens your self-esteem.

You identified ways you blame, criticize, or compare yourself. You learned how to change a shaming inner voice into a positive, self-affirming inner voice. Having compassionate and respectful inner voices is the key to self-esteem.

And you learned to combine the I-Did-It List with Changing Your Inner Voices to build positive self-esteem.

Before the next session, read pages 109 through 132 in *Stick Up for Yourself!* If necessary, tell students where and when the next session will be.

SESSION 10: BUILDING INNER SECURITY

Reading Assignment
Stick Up for Yourself! pages 109–132

In **session 10**, students learn that inner security is about feeling safe in the world as well as secure inside themselves. To build inner security, students learn to recognize two challenges that undermine safety and security: powerlessness and uncertainty. Because powerlessness and uncertainty are always part of life for everyone, students learn to identify these conditions in everyday situations. Students also learn there are limits to how much power and certainty is actually possible. This means they must learn to live with at least some degree of powerlessness and also with a degree of uncertainty. Students acquire important new tools for combating fear and worrying, and learn how to protect themselves when texting anyone or visiting social media sites online. Students also think about things they can begin doing every day to be good to themselves and take care of themselves.

Learner Outcomes
The purpose of this session is to help students:

- understand the power scale
- understand the certainty scale
- learn to accept limits on power and certainty and to live with some powerlessness and uncertainty
- learn how to locate their position on each scale in various situations and how to use this information
- demonstrate through role-plays new ways to handle fear and worrying
- learn how to use the five tools discussed in the reading assignment for today: Active Imagination; Create a Door in Your Mind; Use Your Imagination to Let Go and Feel Calm; Reach Out and Care for Others; and Creating a Personal Shield
- Review four other tools for building inner security: Talking It Over with Yourself; Check Your Position on Your Personal Scales; Look for Choices; and Name and Claim

Materials
- copies of the student book *Stick Up for Yourself!*
- student journals
- the scenarios "Coping with Fear and Worrying" students wrote in Session 9 (you collected these at the end of the session), plus a box or bag to put them in
- copies of the "Six Good Things to Do for Yourself" handout (page 106)
- *optional:* copies of the "Role-Playing Scenarios: Coping with Fear and Worrying" handout (page 107)
- board or flip chart

Agenda

1. Introduce the session.
2. Lead the discussion "Two Scales: Power and Certainty."
3. Lead the activity "Using Your Personal Scales: Finding Your Position."
4. Lead a discussion about the five new tools for building inner security.
5. Lead the role-play activity "Coping with Fear and Worrying," in which students help each other handle fear and worrying more effectively.
6. Assign the activity "Six Good Things to Do for Yourself" as homework for the next session.
7. Have students write role-play scenarios focusing on power and choice with other people to be used in the final session.
8. Close the session.

ACTIVITY AND DISCUSSION

1. Introduction

Say: **In this session, we'll learn more about the two scales you read about in your assigned reading for today, and we'll see how they connect to inner security. The first scale is the power scale. The second is the certainty scale. We'll learn how to use these scales to guide us through different situations. We'll also learn how to use other tools for building our inner security. And we'll role-play ways to deal with fear and worrying.**

2. Two Scales: Power and Certainty

Write "Power" up high on the board or flip chart. Ask: **Who remembers from your reading what *power* is? Who can define it for us?** *(Power is about being in control, being able to control events, having power over something or someone, or having the power to make something happen that you want to happen.)* To the left of the word *power*, write "Lots of Control" as the definition.

Write "Certainty" up high on the board or flip chart, to the right of "Power," leaving space between them. Ask: **Who remembers what *certainty* is? Who can define that for us?** *(Certainty is about being able to predict events and knowing that something that you expect to happen will actually happen. When you're certain, there's no doubt in your mind.)* Beside the word *certainty* and to the right, write "Predictable" and "Little Doubt" as the definition.

Say: **Would someone give us an example of power? Now an example of certainty?** Write the two examples either beside or under each word's definition, depending on the space you have. You want your students to be able to see the connection between these ideas. If students need help getting started, ask: **Do you have power over deciding which clothes you wear to school? Are you certain that the sun will rise each morning?**

Write "Powerlessness" below "Power," leaving some space between the words. Ask: **What about *powerlessness*? Would someone define that?** *(Powerlessness is the opposite of power. It means being out of control, being helpless, having almost no power to make something happen that you want to happen.)* To the left of the word *powerlessness*, write "Little or No Control" as the definition.

Note: When you've completed the writing on the board or chart for this activity, "Power" and "Powerlessness" will be lined up in a vertical column, with their definitions and examples to the left of the column. You'll create a similar pattern with "Certainty" and "Uncertainty," and their definitions and examples will be on the right. See page 99 for a diagram of how this will look.

Write "Uncertainty" below "Certainty." Ask: **And how about *uncertainty*? Can someone define that for us?** *(Uncertainty is the opposite of certainty. It means something is unpredictable. It means not being able to know or predict what will happen, or not being able to count on something or someone. When you're uncertain, there's always doubt.)* To the right of the word *uncertainty*, write "Unpredictable" and "Lots of Doubt" as the definition.

Ask: **Who can give an example of powerlessness? What can't you control?** If students need help, provide a prompt such as: **Are you powerless over whether you have to go to school?**

Ask: **Who can give an example of uncertainty? What can't you predict with confidence?** Again, if students need guidance, offer a prompt such as: **How certain can you be about your score on a surprise math quiz?**

Here's approximately what your diagram should look like:

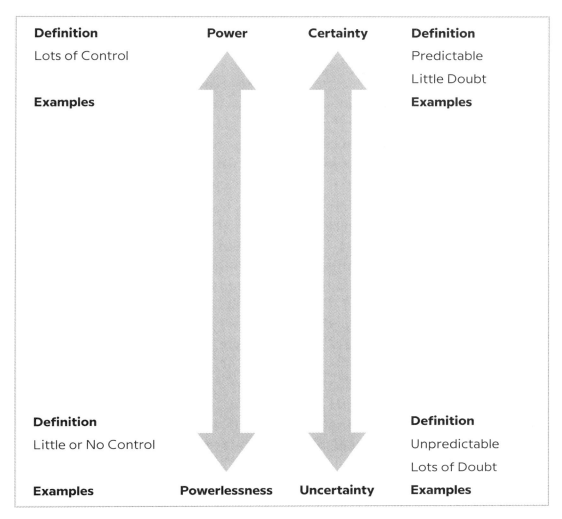

Ask: **Does everyone understand these ideas and how they relate to each other?** Answer questions as needed.

Ask: **Can you ever have total power? Can you ever have total control? Can you always predict what will happen with certainty? Or are there real limits on power and also on certainty? Who can give an example of having either more power or less power?**

How about having more certainty or less certainty?

How do you feel when you're uncertain in a situation? Who can give us an example?

How do you feel when you're powerless in a situation? Who can give us an example of that?

Ask: **What can you do when you're powerless?** (*You want them to say: Look for choices and make choices.*)

How about when you're uncertain about something important and whether it will happen the way you expect? What can you do then? (*You want them to say: Look for choices that are realistic and whose outcomes you can predict. You may need to help students distinguish between what's realistic and what's unrealistic.*)

Say: **Now I'm drawing two vertical lines on the board, one connecting power with powerlessness, and the other connecting certainty with uncertainty. Turn to 117 in your book to follow along with me. Power is at the top of one scale, and certainty is at the top of the second scale. Powerlessness and uncertainty are at the bottom of these two scales. Think of these as your** *personal scales*—**your** *personal guides.*

Who has ever used a compass to find your way or determine your location? Or watched a compass being used for this purpose? How does a compass work? Anyone? *(You want students to say a compass is used for navigation; it helps you find out where you are.)*

Point to the scales on the board or flip chart and say: **You can use these two scales like you would use a compass. Think of them as a tool for locating your position in any situation you find yourself in.**

Ask: **Can someone tell us how to use these scales? Would you give an example? Now someone else?** If they need help, say: **Imagine your best friend suddenly stops talking to you and won't even reply to your text messages. Now picture these two scales. Where are you located on each scale in this situation?**

Go around the group until everyone who wants to share has given an example. Then ask: **How do you feel when you're at the top of either scale? At the bottom? How about when you're in the middle?**

Ask: **Who has some examples of being at the top, middle, and bottom of each of these scales?** Write these examples on the board beside each scale position, and then write down the feelings your students experience at each scale position. This shows the connection between scale position and various feelings. Allow about 15 minutes for this activity.

(If you don't have sufficient room on the board or flip chart for these examples, use another board or a separate page in your flip chart. Be sure the diagram with the two scales remains visible for the rest of the session.)

3. Using Your Personal Scales: Finding Your Position

Now, divide the group into six small groups roughly equal in size. Position these groups around the room, with three lined up along one wall and the other three lined up along the opposite wall. The three groups along one wall represent the *power scale,* and the three groups along the other wall represent the *certainty scale.*

Spread out the three groups representing the power scale along their wall and tell them their groups represent, in turn, being very high, in the middle, or very low on that scale. Likewise, spread out the three groups representing the certainty scale along the other wall and tell them they represent, in turn, being very high, in the middle, or very low on that scale. Remind them that being high on the scale means experiencing greater power or greater certainty, while being low means experiencing greater powerlessness or greater uncertainty.

Make sure everyone understands which scale position their group represents. Tell each group to pick a situation that depicts the particular scale position they are representing. It could be a situation they've experienced in their lives, witnessed on TV, heard about, or read about. Allow a few minutes for each group to discuss the scale and scale position they represent and then to agree on a situation.

Say: **I want you all to come up with ways to deal with either powerlessness or uncertainty, depending on the group you're in and your scale position. If you're in a group that represents being high on the power or certainty scale, remember that you can never have** *total* **power or** *total* **certainty.** Allow several minutes for this activity.

Say: **Now, would someone from each group volunteer to tell us about the situation your group chose and how you decided to handle it?**

After someone has spoken from each group, say: **Would someone from the power scale set of groups tell us how your group's position on the scale connects to inner security?**

Now would someone from the certainty scale set of groups tell us how your group's position on the scale connects to inner security?

Allow five minutes for discussion. Then bring the students back together in their original seats. The entire activity should take about 15 to 20 minutes, though you can allow more time if you have it.

4. Tools for Building Inner Security

Note: You could allow more time for discussion of the following tools depending on how much time the other activities take and how much overall time you have available. You could also focus the discussion on just two or three of these tools and give them more consideration.

Active Imagination

Say: **In the assigned reading for today, you read about several new tools. Can anyone tell us what the first one was?** *(Active imagination.)* **How does it work? Can someone volunteer to describe it? In which situations would you use active imagination?** *(When worried or fearful.)*

Ask: **Do you think active imagination would help you handle a bullying situation? How? Would someone volunteer to say how to use it in this situation?** *(Imagine the scene and then imagine one of your fears or worries actually happening. Finally, imagine how you'd deal with it.)*

Ask: **What if you felt scared about something dangerous happening to you? Or you felt personally threatened by violence? How could you use active imagination in these situations?**

Create a Door in Your Mind

Ask: Would someone describe what Create a Door in Your Mind is and how to use it? How about another volunteer? Has anyone tried it since you first read about it?

In what situations would you use it?

Does anyone here worry? Occasionally? Often? A lot? Would anyone like to tell us what you worry about? Anyone else?

Note: If you are concerned about a student who worries a very great deal, discuss this with your school counselor or school principal.

Ask: How would you use this tool to stop worrying?

Use Your Imagination to Let Go and Feel Calm

Ask: Would someone describe what Use Your Imagination to Let Go and Feel Calm is and how to use it? How about another volunteer? Has anyone tried it since you first read about it? How did it work for you?

In what situations would you use this tool?

Reach Out and Care for Others

Say: We first talked about caring for others in session 7 (pages 68–76) when we learned about the need to nurture others. Caring for others is also another way to help us build inner security.

Ask: Has anyone been kind or helpful to someone else recently? A friend? A family member? How about a neighbor? Have students brainstorm ideas for helping others or caring for others. Spend a few minutes on this, and write the ideas on the board or chart.

End the discussion of this tool by asking: **How does caring for others help *you*?** Write students' thoughts and ideas on the board or flip chart.

Creating a Personal Shield

Ask: Can anyone tell us about the last new tool described in your reading assignment? What was it? *(Creating a personal shield.)* **How does it work? When would you use it?**

Ask: Does anyone use a computer, tablet, or smartphone? If so, do you ever use it to visit social media websites online? Which ones do you visit? How do you feel after you've been online?

How could you use your Personal Shield when you visit social media sites? How about when you text friends or family? How do you think it could be helpful?

End the activity by saying: **Take some time to reread today's assigned reading with an adult you trust, and then talk it over together.**

We can also learn from seeing how other people handle difficult feelings like fear and worrying. Let's do that next.

5. Role-Plays: Coping with Fear and Worrying

Say: **In the last session, each of you wrote about something that's happening in your life—a situation involving fear or worrying.**

Note: If you didn't have time in session 9 for students to write scenarios, hand out copies of "Role-Playing Scenarios: Coping with Fear and Worrying" (page 107). Assign a scenario to each pair, or let students choose the ones they want to do.

We're going to role-play some of those situations now so we can learn from each other.

Divide the class into pairs. Each pair will do at least one role-play—or more, depending on the size of your group and how much time you have available.

Ask someone from each pair to come up and draw a piece of paper (with a role-playing scenario written on it) from the box or bag.

When every pair has a scenario, say: **In these role-plays, one member of each pair will describe a situation you're fearful or frightened of or a situation you worry a lot about.**

Then the other member of that pair will offer specific tools for how to better handle those feelings, how to counteract them, or how to reduce them. You can use any of the tools for dealing with fear and worrying you've read about in your reading assignment. You can refer to your books if you need reminders. When you're describing tools to your partner and to the class, be sure to demonstrate how to use one of the tools. Show us how to use it as well as you can.

Now read about the situation you will role-play and decide who will play which role. You'll have several minutes to rehearse.

Bring the class back together and ask for volunteers to go first. Tell them to read the scenario out loud first and then do the role-play.

After the role-play, ask the class: **What ideas did you get from this role-play? Do you understand what you can do to feel less fearful or worried? What's clear? What isn't clear?**

Allow time for discussion. Then thank the first pair and ask for volunteers to go second.

Continue with this process—role-play followed by discussion—until all pairs have participated. Then ask the large group: **Did you learn at least one new way to reduce fear? One new way to manage worrying? When and where do you think you might try it?**

End the activity by saying: **We can all be role models for each other. We can learn a lot from seeing how others handle difficult situations. We can help one another cope better, deal more effectively with uncertainty and powerlessness, and teach each other tools for building self-esteem and inner security.**

You still have to make your own decisions because only you are responsible for your own feelings and behavior. But it always helps to get ideas from other people.

6. Six Good Things to Do for Yourself

Hand out copies of "Six Good Things to Do for Yourself." Then say: **This is your homework assignment. When you get home, read the six good things at the top of this sheet. Then fill in the blanks at the bottom.**

Do as many of these good things as you can before the next session. Bring your sheet to the session. We'll talk about it then.

If you need ideas, look at pages 107 and 108 of *Stick Up for Yourself!*

7. Writing a Role-Play Scenario: Power and Choice with Other People

Note: If you don't have time for this writing activity but you still want to do the role-playing in session 11, you can use the ideas on the "Role-Playing Scenarios: Power and Choice with Other People" handout (page 115).

Hand out sheets of paper. Say: **In all these sessions, you've been learning new ways to stick up for yourself. Next week, you're going to role-play ways to stick up for yourself with others, using your own ideas.**

Write about something that's happening in your life—a situation in which you'd like to stick up for yourself. Don't sign your name. Just describe the situation.

If students have trouble thinking of something to write, give a few examples:

- A kid at school teases you all the time.
- Your sister takes the remote when you're watching TV.
- Your dad makes you go to bed at 8:00 every night, and you think that's too early.
- Your soccer coach yells at you—especially if you make a mistake—and belittles you in front of the whole team.
- A kid in your class bullies you on the playground.

Give students time to write, then collect their papers. End the activity by saying: **Next week, we'll role-play as many of these as we have time for. This will give you new ideas about how to stick up for yourself.**

8. Closing

Summarize by saying: **In this session you learned about two scales: power and certainty. You learned how to find your position on each scale in any situation you face. And you learned five new tools for building inner security: Active Imagination; Create a Door in Your Mind; Use Your Imagination to Let Go and Feel Calm; Reach Out and Care for Others; and Creating a Personal Shield. Now you have lots of tools to boost your inner security.**

Here are some more reminders: Whenever you're powerless or uncertain in a situation, remember to talk it over with yourself—just like you learned to do with feelings, dreams, and needs in earlier sessions.

Then find your position on each of your personal scales. Always ask yourself these questions:

Am I high, low, or in the middle on the power scale?

Am I high, low, or in the middle on the certainty scale?

Ask yourself, "How do I feel about my position on each scale? What can I do about it?"

Also, remember to look for choices. *(Choice = power.)*

And remember to name and claim. *(Feelings, dreams, and needs.)*

Say: **Before the next session, be sure to do your homework. Fill in the "Six Good Things to Do for Yourself" sheet, try some of your ideas—you can start today—and bring the sheet with you to the next session.**

The next session will be our last session for this course.

If necessary, tell students where and when the next session will be.

Before the Next Session

During the final session, you'll ask students to complete a course evaluation. (See "About the Evaluations" on pages 6–7.) You might use the form on pages 118–119, or you might prefer to create your own evaluation. You'll need to decide in advance so you'll have copies available to hand out next time.

If you want to ask parents or caregivers to evaluate the course, you can either use the form on pages 120–121 or create your own. Have copies ready for the next session if you want to send them home with students.

STICK UP FOR YOURSELF!

SIX GOOD THINGS TO DO FOR YOURSELF

1. Choose something to do just for fun. Then do it whenever you can.
2. Give yourself a treat every day. This can be almost anything, as long as it's just for you.
3. Forgive yourself for something you did in the past.
4. Do at least one thing every day that's good for your body.
5. Do at least one thing every day that's good for your brain.
6. Find adults you can trust and talk to. Let your feelings guide you to the right people. Pick three or more you feel safe with. Pick those who care enough to listen and try to understand how you feel.

MY PLAN

I'll do this just for fun:
_____

I'll give myself this treat:
_____

I'll forgive myself for:
_____

I'll do this for my body:
_____

I'll do this for my brain:
_____

These are adults I can trust and talk to:
_____
_____
_____

From *A Teacher's Guide to Stick Up for Yourself!* by Gershen Kaufman, Ph.D., and Lev Raphael, Ph.D., copyright © 2019. This page may be reproduced for individual, classroom, or small group work only. For other uses, contact www.freespirit.com/permissions.

STICK UP FOR YOURSELF!

ROLE-PLAYING SCENARIOS: COPING WITH FEAR AND WORRYING

1. You're scared about hurricanes, flooding, or tornadoes.

2. You always worry for days before a big math exam.

3. You worry a lot about school shootings, or shootings at churches, mosques, or synagogues.

4. When you have to give a speech in class, you're up worrying the whole night beforehand.

5. You're really scared about standing up to bullying.

6. You're afraid to talk to people you don't know.

7. You worry all the time about poverty, world hunger, or climate change.

8. When your parents argue, you feel very frightened.

9. You feel terrified when you think about the possibility of a terrorist attack.

10. You're anxious about whether you'll be able to finish all your schoolwork.

11. Your coach or teacher has been unfair to you, but you're scared to talk to him or her about it.

12. You're very scared because you feel unsafe in your home, school, or neighborhood.

From *A Teacher's Guide to Stick Up for Yourself!* by Gershen Kaufman, Ph.D., and Lev Raphael, Ph.D., copyright © 2019. This page may be reproduced for individual, classroom, or small group work only. For other uses, contact www.freespirit.com/permissions.

SESSION 11: STICKING UP FOR YOURSELF FROM NOW ON: REVIEWING YOUR CHOICES

Session 11 reviews the ways students have been learning to stick up for themselves. Through role-play, students are able to demonstrate their understanding of the various tools they can use to stick up for themselves.

Learner Outcomes

The purpose of this session is to help students:

- review tools they learned to use in this course: the Happiness List, the I-Did-It List, Talking Things Over with Yourself, Change Your Inner Voices, Active Imagination, and Creating a Personal Shield
- demonstrate through role-plays ways to stick up for themselves with other people
- evaluate their progress toward their goals, which they described in writing in session 1
- evaluate the course as a whole

Materials

- copies of the student book *Stick Up for Yourself!*
- student journals
- students' completed "Six Good Things to Do for Yourself" homework assignments from session 10 (students should bring these)
- the scenarios students wrote in session 10 (you collected these at the end of the session); a box or bag to put them in
- *optional:* copies of the "Scripts for Talking Things Over with Yourself" handout (pages 116–117)
- *optional:* copies of the "Role-Playing Scenarios: Power and Choice with Other People" handout (page 115)
- copies of the "Student Course Evaluation" (pages 118–119) or your own evaluation form
- *optional:* copies of the "Parent and Caregiver Course Evaluation" (pages 120–121) or your own evaluation form

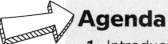

Agenda

1. Introduce the session.
2. Review the "Six Good Things to Do for Yourself" homework assignment from session 10.
3. Lead the discussion "Our Lists—Another Look."
4. Lead the activity "Keep Talking Things Over with Yourself."
5. Lead the activity "Keep Listening to and Changing Your Inner Voices."
6. Lead the activity "One New Thing I Do to Stick Up for Myself."
7. Lead the role-play activity "Power and Choice with Other People," in which students help each other identify ways to stick up for themselves.
8. Ask students to do a self-evaluation of their progress in the course. They will read the goals that they wrote during session 1 and decide whether they met their goals.
9. Ask students to evaluate the course as a whole.
10. Close the session.

ACTIVITY AND DISCUSSION

1. Introduction

Say: **In this final session, we'll review some of the things we've learned together. We'll also do some role-playing to help each other find new ways to stick up for ourselves.**

2. Six Good Things to Do for Yourself

Say: **In the last session, you had a homework assignment. Let's find out how that went. Take out your "Six Good Things to Do for Yourself" assignment sheets.**

Ask: **Who would like to tell us what you did just for fun?**

Which of you gave yourselves a treat? Would you like to tell us what you gave yourself? Was it hard to think of a treat to give yourself every day? How might you make it easier?

Who wants to talk about forgiving yourself for something you did in the past? Was this hard to do? Why do you think it's important to forgive yourself?

What did you do that was good for your body? Did anyone decide to eat differently? Get more sleep? Exercise?

How did you take care of your brain? Did you find something new to read, or think about, or look at, or listen to each day?

Maybe you found an adult to talk to—someone who could help you answer some questions or who was willing to listen to something that was on your mind. Does anyone have anything to say about that?

End the activity by saying: **Remember, one way to stick up for yourself is to take good care of yourself. The way we take care of ourselves one day might be different from what we do the next day. What counts is to keep at it. This is something that will be important throughout your entire life.**

3. Our Lists—Another Look

Say: **We can teach ourselves to notice things we do and feel proud of. What's one thing we learned to do that helps us notice and take credit for what we do each day?** *(You want students to mention the I-Did-It List. If necessary, you can guide them toward this answer.)*

Why is it important to collect good feelings? How can we do that? *(You want students to talk about the Happiness List.)*

Don't forget, your lists are important. Keep adding to them. Your Happiness List is a great way to collect and store positive feelings inside you. Your I-Did-It List is your self-esteem savings account.

What if you have a feeling you want to collect, or you do something you're proud of, but you don't have your journal with you to write it down? *(STOP everything and notice it; FEEL the happy or proud feeling; STORE it inside you; WRITE it down as soon as you can.)*

Even if you don't carry your journal around all the time, you could stick a piece of paper in your pocket to use for your lists. If you keep a tablet or smartphone with you, you can use that for your lists if you prefer.

Encourage students to find notebooks they can carry and use throughout the day (unless they'd rather use smartphones or tablets). You may want to show them some small notebooks—maybe some you have used to keep your own lists. Or show them sheets of paper you've written on. Tell them there are many kinds of small notebooks they can easily carry in a pocket, school bag, or backpack.

Say: **Plan your time so you can review your lists during the last few minutes before you go to sleep every night. Feel the happy and proud feelings all over again.**

Now and then, read through your lists and enjoy your good feelings again. Or pick something to experience all over again.

4. Keep Talking Things Over with Yourself

Note: As you lead this activity, you may want to refer to the "Talk Things Over with Yourself" scripts from pages 60–61 of the student book, *Stick Up for Yourself!* To avoid having to flip through the book, you can also use the "Scripts for Talking Things Over with Yourself" handout on pages 116–117 of this guide.

Say: **What can we talk over with ourselves?** *(Feelings, needs, and dreams.)*

Can anyone tell me how we can talk things over with ourselves? Let's start with feelings. How can we talk over a feeling with ourselves? How can we start? What question can we ask? *(How am I feeling today?)*

After you name the feeling, what can you ask? Find the script in your journal, if you need help remembering. *(When you know the feeling, you ask, "Why am I feeling_____? What's happened that I feel_____ about?" Then ask what you can do about the feeling.)*

Follow this same discussion pattern to review the process of talking over needs and dreams with yourself.

Say: **Also remember to talk things over with yourself whenever you're feeling powerless or uncertain.**

End the activity by saying: **You can't always find someone else to talk to, even when you really need to talk. But you can always talk things over with yourself. This will help you understand your feelings, your dreams, and your needs better and give you choices for what to do about them.**

5. Keep Listening to and Changing Your Inner Voices

Say: **In session 9, you learned to *listen to* your inner voices. Then you learned how to *change* your inner voices. Can anyone remember what we learned about *inner voices*?**

What do you remember about shaming inner voices? What do they feel like inside and what are the words these voices say to you? *(They're blaming, critical, and comparing.)*

Has anyone tried to change an inner voice since we met last time? How do we change shaming inner voices into self-affirming inner voices? *(New words, new feelings, imagining a new voice speaking inside.)*

End the activity by saying: **Remember, changing your inner voices will take time and practice. Just listening to your inner voices is an important first step. So remember to pay close attention to how you behave toward yourself and how you talk to yourself.**

6. One New Thing I Do to Stick Up for Myself

Say: **I'm going to go around the room. I'd like each of you to tell me one new thing you're doing to stick up for yourself** *with other people.*

Give each student a chance to contribute. Then say: **Now I'm going to go around the room again. I'd like each of you to tell me one new thing you're doing to stick up for yourself** *with yourself.*

If students have trouble with this, you might ask: **Are you doing anything differently when you make a mistake?**

Congratulate students for sticking up for themselves. Then say: **Keep noticing ways you're sticking up for yourself. Tell yourself you're doing a good job. Take time now and then to look in a mirror, into your own eyes, and say to yourself: "I'm good enough just the way I am."**

You can also learn from watching how other people stick up for themselves. Let's do that next.

7. Role-Plays: Power and Choice with Other People

Say: **In the last session, you each wrote about something that's happening in your life—a situation where you'd like to stick up for yourself.**

Note: If you didn't have time in session 10 for students to write scenarios, hand out copies of "Role-Playing Scenarios: Power and Choice with Other People." Assign a scenario to each pair, or let students choose the ones they want to do.

Say: **We're going to role-play some of those situations so we can learn from each other. In these role-plays, one member of each pair will describe the situation. Then the other member of that pair will offer specific tools for how to better handle the situation.**

Divide the class into pairs. Each pair will do at least one role-play—or more, depending on the size of your group and how much time you have available.

Ask someone from each pair to come up and draw a piece of paper (with a role-playing scenario on it) from the box or bag. When every pair has a scenario, say: **Read about the situation you will role-play, then decide who plays which role. You'll have a few minutes to rehearse.**

After several minutes, bring the class back together and ask for volunteers to go first. Tell them to read the scenario out loud, then do the role-play.

After each role-play, ask the class: **What ideas did you get from this role-play? Do you understand what you might do to stick up for yourself in this situation or one like it? What's clear? What isn't clear?**

Allow time for discussion. Then thank the first pair and ask for volunteers to go second.

Continue with this process—role-play, then discussion—until all pairs have participated. Then ask the class: **Did you learn at least one new way to stick up for yourself? Where do you think you might try it?**

End the activity by saying: **Remember, we can all be role models for each other. We can all learn from one another. But we still have to make our own decisions. That's because each of us is responsible for our own feelings and behavior. Still, it helps to get ideas from others.**

8. Student Self-Evaluation

Say: **During the first session, you each set a goal for yourself. You described it in writing in your journal. Now I want you to find that page in your notebook.**

You wrote an ending to this sentence:

> In these sessions, I want to learn new ways to stick up for myself when . . .

Take a few minutes and write, on the same page, any new ways you've learned to stick up for yourself. This is just for you; you don't need to share it with anyone else.

Ask: **How many of you think you met your goal?**

Remind students that change takes time. Even if they aren't yet where they want to be, they're learning and growing. That's success.

9. Student Course Evaluation

Hand out copies of the "Student Course Evaluation" or your own evaluation form. Say: **I want to find out how you feel about these sessions and this course as a whole. I'm going to give you a form to fill out. Please tell me what you want me to know about your experience. It will help me when I teach this course to another group of students. If you need more room to write, you can use the back of the sheet.**

Give students a few minutes to complete the evaluation. Be sure to collect the forms before students leave the room.

> ### Optional **Parent and Caregiver Course Evaluation**
> If you want to ask parents and caregivers to evaluate the course, you can give students copies of the "Parent and Caregiver Course Evaluation" to take home with them, or you can email or mail the form to families directly.

10. Closing

Summarize by saying: In these sessions, you learned new ways to strengthen your self-esteem and to stick up for yourself. You learned how to increase your personal power and how to build inner security. You have tools you can use every day, starting today. Those tools include:

- The Happiness List
- The I-Did-It List
- Talking Things Over with Yourself
- Change Your Inner Voices
- Active Imagination
- Creating a Personal Shield

Say: Thank you for your part—for sharing your feelings and thoughts and for helping each other learn new ways to stick up for yourselves.

Remember, change takes time. Keep practicing the tools you've learned until they become automatic—until they are a part of you.

You can continue developing personal power, positive self-esteem, and inner security for the rest of your lives. Keep sticking up for yourself with others—and with yourself.

STICK UP FOR YOURSELF!

ROLE-PLAYING SCENARIOS: POWER AND CHOICE WITH OTHER PEOPLE

1. You're at a movie and the kid behind you is loud and annoying.

2. A teacher doesn't give you the full directions for an assignment, so you don't get a good grade.

3. Your parents blame you for something you didn't do.

4. Your parents break a promise they made to you.

5. A friend says that your entry in a contest was dumb.

6. Someone in your class always bugs you and calls you names.

7. Someone teases you about the boy or girl you like.

8. Your friends plan to get even with someone who did something they didn't like. You tell your friends you want to stay out of it, but they get mad at you.

9. The teacher asks a question but won't call on you when you raise your hand.

10. Your coach doesn't give your team any credit for trying.

11. A kid at school picks on you and bullies you.

12. A friend reveals a secret you shared online.

STICK UP FOR YOURSELF!

SCRIPTS FOR TALKING THINGS OVER WITH YOURSELF

You can use the following examples to get started when you're talking with yourself about your feelings, future dreams, and needs.

FEELINGS

Ask yourself, "How am I feeling today?" Then name a feeling you're having. Next, talk it over with yourself. Your talk might go something like this:

Say: "I'm feeling sad today."

Ask: "Why am I feeling sad? What's happened that I feel sad about?"

Say: "I'm feeling sad because I had an argument with my dad last night."

Ask: "What can I do about my sad feeling?"

Say: "I can talk to my dad about the argument."

FUTURE DREAMS

Ask yourself, "What are my future dreams?" Then name a dream for the near future or the far future. Next, talk it over with yourself. Your talk might go something like this:

Say: "I want to work with animals someday."

Ask: "What do I have to learn to make this dream happen?"

Say: "I can start by reading books about people who work with animals."

Ask: "What else can I do?"

Say: "I can talk to veterinarians and animal trainers."

From *A Teacher's Guide to Stick Up for Yourself!* by Gershen Kaufman, Ph.D., and Lev Raphael, Ph.D., copyright © 2019. This page may be reproduced for individual, classroom, or small group work only. For other uses, contact www.freespirit.com/permissions.

Scripts for Talking Things Over with Yourself continued

NEEDS

Ask yourself, "What do I need right now?" Try to name your need. Then talk it over with yourself. Your talk might go something like this:

Say: "I need to make friends at school. I feel left out and lonely sometimes."

Ask: "How can I start making friends?"

Say: "I can ask if anyone wants to play a game with me at recess."

Ask: "What if nobody says yes?"

Say: "I can find another group of kids who are playing games. I can ask if it's okay to join them."

TIPS FOR TALKING THINGS OVER WITH YOURSELF

- Try to make this a habit. Set aside time to do it every day.

- Talk out loud to yourself if you have a private place you can go to. If not, write down your questions and answers in a notebook or tablet. Or just think them.

STICK UP FOR YOURSELF!

STUDENT COURSE EVALUATION

1. I am keeping a Happiness List . . . *(choose one answer)*
   ☐ every day   ☐ most days   ☐ now and then   ☐ never

2. I am keeping an I-Did-It List . . .
   ☐ every day   ☐ most days   ☐ now and then   ☐ never

3. One way I learned to stick up for myself is . . . *(write your answer)*

4. I am talking *feelings* over with myself . . .
   ☐ every day   ☐ most days   ☐ now and then   ☐ never

5. I am talking *dreams* over with myself . . .
   ☐ every day   ☐ most days   ☐ now and then   ☐ never

6. I am talking *needs* over with myself . . .
   ☐ every day   ☐ most days   ☐ now and then   ☐ never

7. I am more aware of my inner voices…
   ☐ every day   ☐ most days   ☐ now and then   ☐ never

8. The tool that helped me most in this course was . . .
   ☐ The Happiness List   ☐ The I-Did-It List
   ☐ Talking Things Over with Yourself   ☐ Changing Your Inner Voices
   ☐ Active Imagination   ☐ Creating a Personal Shield

From *A Teacher's Guide to Stick Up for Yourself!* by Gershen Kaufman, Ph.D., and Lev Raphael, Ph.D., copyright © 2019. This page may be reproduced for individual, classroom, or small group work only. For other uses, contact www.freespirit.com/permissions.

Student Course Evaluation continued

9. The thing I learned the most about in this course was . . . *(write your answer)*

10. I wish there had been more _____ in this course.

11. I wish there had been less _____ in this course.

12. Do you have any other comments or suggestions? Write them here.

From *A Teacher's Guide to Stick Up for Yourself!* by Gershen Kaufman, Ph.D., and Lev Raphael, Ph.D., copyright © 2019. This page may be reproduced for individual, classroom, or small group work only. For other uses, contact www.freespirit.com/permissions.

STICK UP FOR YOURSELF!

PARENT AND CAREGIVER COURSE EVALUATION

1. Have you observed any changes in your child's behavior since he or she began taking this course? In particular, is there anything you have noticed that makes you think your child is developing new ways to stick up for himself or herself?

    ☐ yes   ☐ no

    If you feel comfortable doing so, please describe what you have observed.

2. Did your child bring home the book *Stick Up for Yourself! Every Kid's Guide to Personal Power and Positive Self-Esteem* and give you a chance to read it?

    ☐ yes   ☐ no

3. Did you read the book too?

    ☐ yes   ☐ no

4. Did your child talk with you about what we were discussing in the course?

    ☐ every day   ☐ most days   ☐ now and then   ☐ never

5. Did your child tell you about the Happiness List and the I-Did-It List we were keeping?

    ☐ yes   ☐ no

6. Did your child tell you about using Active Imagination and Creating a Personal Shield?

    ☐ yes   ☐ no

7. Did your child tell you about learning how to handle fear and worrying?

    ☐ yes   ☐ no

From *A Teacher's Guide to Stick Up for Yourself!* by Gershen Kaufman, Ph.D., and Lev Raphael, Ph.D., copyright © 2019. This page may be reproduced for individual, classroom, or small group work only. For other uses, contact www.freespirit.com/permissions.

Parent and Caregiver Course Evaluation continued

8. Does your child seem more confident and secure after having taken this course?

    ☐ yes ☐ no

9. Do you feel that this course was a good experience for your child? Why or why not?

10. When we teach the course again, what do you think we should tell parents, caregivers, and families about it?

11. Do you have any other comments or suggestions?

Please return this form to _____ *by*
(name)

_____ .
(date)

ADDITIONAL ACTIVITIES ACROSS THE CURRICULUM

CURRICULUM-RELATED ACTIVITIES

The activities in this section allow you to reinforce the concepts students are learning in this course. They are related to curriculum areas.

Language Arts and Creative Writing

1. In a book or story, ask students to find examples of ways the writer lets us know what the characters are feeling. Give these examples:

   - *He looked down at the ground as he walked. His hands were in his pockets.*
     What might he be feeling? Why?

   - *She was practically skipping down the hall.*
     What might she be feeling? Why?

   - *John looked at his test results and said, "Oh, yes!"*
     What might John be feeling? Why?

2. Ask students to write a paragraph that describes a feeling, without naming the feeling.

Social Studies

1. Ask students to find photographs of people in newspapers, in magazines, and online. Ask them to identify what they think the people in the pictures might have been feeling when the picture was taken.

2. Tell students that politicians know that one way to get public support is to get people's feelings involved in an issue. Ask them to watch the evening news to try to find an example in which a politician may have been trying to "trigger" a certain feeling. Ask them to tell what the politician said that made them think it was an attempt to get people to feel a certain way about an issue.

3. Find headlines in newspapers, in magazines, or online that use names of feelings or that describe or convey feelings.

4. Have students research how people from various cultures express their feelings.

Art

To help students learn how to draw nonverbal clues that show emotions, ask them how they would draw inanimate objects so they look like they have feelings. Divide them into groups, and ask them to come up with ideas. *Examples:* A joyful pencil, a sad house, an excited table, a furious lamp.

Film and Television

Show a video or film clip with the sound turned off. Have students watch faces shown in the clip and then try to name the feelings displayed. Use the list of feelings on page 25 of the student book. You might also include the combined feelings (contempt, jealousy, loneliness, down mood) described on pages 40–46.

Music

Ask students to bring in recordings of songs that always make them feel happy. Preview the songs, then use appropriate songs as background music during another group activity.

Other Languages

Have students translate the names of feelings into another language that they are studying or would like to study. Tell them to make a poster showing each word in English and in as many other languages as they can find.

SOCIAL ACTIVITIES

An important part of this course is the social interaction among students. During the course, you may want to arrange social activities that extend beyond the regular session time. This section presents some ideas for doing this.

Breaks

- During breaks, encourage students to get to know someone in class they don't already know.
- Tell students you will have a "Spotlight Minute" after the break. This can be a signal that anyone in the group can tell something interesting they learned about someone else during the break.

Phone Calls and Texting

When students are making new friends, they sometimes find it scary to make phone calls to each other. Have each student exchange phone numbers with one other person. During the week, they should text each other to say "Hello!" or "How's it going?" and also call at least once. Have them decide who will call first. Ask them to think about what they might talk about. Ask them why they sometimes feel nervous about making a phone call or texting. *Examples:* They might think the other person won't be glad to hear from them, or they might be afraid someone else will answer the phone or read their text message.

Parties

Plan a party for the end of the course. Ask volunteers to help plan it. Ask the volunteers to make up a recipe for the party which tells each class member what to bring to the party. *Example:* 1 joke, 1 board game, 1 small can of soda, 2 snacks to share.

RESOURCES

Boost Emotional Intelligence in Students: 30 Flexible Research-Based Activities to Build EQ Skills (Grades 5–9) by Maurice J. Elias, Ph.D., and Steven E. Tobias, Psy.D. (Minneapolis: Free Spirit Publishing, 2018). Explains what emotional intelligence is and why it's important for all students. Lays out detailed yet flexible guidelines for teaching fundamental EQ in an intentional and focused way.

Coming Out of Shame: Transforming Gay and Lesbian Lives by Gershen Kaufman, Ph.D., and Lev Raphael, Ph.D. (New York: Doubleday, 1996). Applies the principles and tools for overcoming shame and developing personal power specifically to sexual orientation and sexual identity.

Dynamics of Power: Fighting Shame and Building Self-Esteem by Gershen Kaufman, Ph.D., and Lev Raphael, Ph.D. (Rochester, VT: Schenkman Books, 1991). Teaches essential skills for building self-esteem; shows how psychological health and self-esteem depend on overcoming shame and developing personal power.

The Formative Five: Fostering Grit, Empathy, and Other Success Skills Every Student Needs by Thomas R. Hoerr (Alexandria, VA: ASCD, 2017). Shows educators how to foster the "formative five" success skills that today's students need: empathy, self-control, integrity, embracing diversity, and grit.

How (and Why) to Get Students Talking: 78 Ready-to-Use Group Discussions About Anxiety, Self-Esteem, Relationships, and More (Grades 6–12) by Jean Sunde Peterson, Ph.D. (Minneapolis: Free Spirit Publishing, 2019). This book's guided conversations are proven ways to reach out to young people and address their social-emotional development, and the discussions can be easily adapted and customized.

"How Are You Feeling Today?" (Cincinnati, OH: Creative Therapy Associates, ctherapy.com). This poster, designed by Jim Borgman, illustrates thirty different feelings, from exhausted to ecstatic, embarrassed to smug.

A Practical Guide to Mental Health & Learning Disorders for Every Educator: How to Recognize, Understand, and Help Challenged (and Challenging) Students Succeed by Myles Cooley, Ph.D. (Minneapolis: Free Spirit Publishing, 2018). Using clear, jargon-free language, this book helps all educators—whether in inclusive classrooms, general education settings, or other environments—recognize mental health issues and learning disabilities that are often observed in students.

The Psychology of Shame: Theory and Treatment of Shame-Based Syndromes by Gershen Kaufman, Ph.D. (New York: Springer Publishing Co., 1996). Expands the theory of shame's role in human development, interpersonal relations, identity formation, and culture.

Shame: The Power of Caring by Gershen Kaufman, Ph.D. (Rochester, VT: Schenkman Books, 1992). Clarifies the role shame plays in all aspects of our lives.

The Six Pillars of Self-Esteem by Nathaniel Branden (New York: Bantam, 1994). Introduces six action-based practices for daily living that provide the foundation for self-esteem and explores the central importance of self-esteem. Provides concrete guidelines for teachers, parents, managers, and therapists who are responsible for developing the self-esteem of others.

Your Perfect Right: Assertiveness and Equality in Your Life and Relationships by Robert E. Alberti, Ph.D., and Michael L. Emmons, Ph.D. (Oakland, CA: Impact Publishers, 2017). The revised and updated edition of a classic guide to equal-relationship assertiveness includes step-by-step procedures, detailed examples, and exercises.

ABOUT THE AUTHORS

Gershen Kaufman was educated at Columbia University and received his Ph.D. in clinical psychology from the University of Rochester. Professor emeritus in psychology at Michigan State University, he is a pioneer in the study of shame. He is the author of *Shame: The Power of Caring* and *The Psychology of Shame: Theory and Treatment of Shame-Based Syndromes*. He is the coauthor with Lev Raphael of *Dynamics of Power: Fighting Shame and Building Self-Esteem* and *Coming Out of Shame: Transforming Gay and Lesbian Lives*. Also with Lev, Gershen codeveloped the program, "Affect and Self-Esteem," on which *Dynamics of Power* and *Stick Up for Yourself!* are based. He lives in Michigan.

Lev Raphael was educated at Fordham University and received his M.F.A. in creative writing from the University of Massachusetts at Amherst. He holds a Ph.D. in English from Michigan State University where he has been an assistant professor in the English Department, teaching literature and creative writing. Lev has authored eight Nick Hoffman mysteries and seventeen other books in many genres and has also blogged for the Huffington Post. You can find Lev online at levraphael.com and writewithoutborders.com. He lives in Michigan.

> To download the reproducible forms from the digital content for this book, visit **freespirit.com/tgsufy-forms**. Use the password **4confidence**.

Other Great Resources from Free Spirit

Stick Up for Yourself!
Every Kid's Guide to Personal Power and Positive Self-Esteem
(Revised & Updated 3rd Edition)
by Gershen Kaufman, Ph.D., and Lev Raphael, Ph.D.

For ages 9–13. 152 pp.; PB; two-color; illust.; 6" x 9".

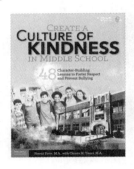

Create a Culture of Kindness in Middle School
48 Character-Building Lessons to Foster Respect and Prevent Bullying
by Naomi Drew, M.A., with Christa M. Tinari, M.A.

For middle school educators. 272 pp.; PB; 8½" x 11"; includes digital content.

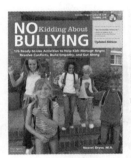

No Kidding About Bullying
126 Ready-to-Use Activities to Help Kids Manage Anger, Resolve Conflicts, Build Empathy, and Get Along (Updated Edition)
by Naomi Drew, M.A.

For educators, grades 3–6. 304 pp.; PB; 8½" x 11"; includes digital content.

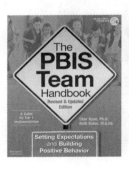

The PBIS Team Handbook
Setting Expectations and Building Positive Behavior (Revised and Updated Edition)
by Char Ryan, Ph.D., and Beth Baker, M.S.Ed.

For K–12 PBIS coaches and team members, including special educators, teachers, paraprofessionals, school psychologists, social workers, counselors, administrators, parents, and other school staff members. 216 pp.; PB; 8½" x 11"; includes digital content.

Bullying Is a Pain in the Brain
(Revised & Updated Edition)
by Trevor Romain, illustrated by Steve Mark

For ages 8–13. 112 pp.; PB; color illust.; 5⅛" x 7".

Cliques, Phonies & Other Baloney
(Revised & Updated Edition)
by Trevor Romain and Elizabeth Verdick, illustrated by Steve Mark

For ages 8–13. 112 pp.; PB; color illust.; 5⅛" x 7".

What to Do When You're Scared & Worried
A Guide for Kids
by James J. Crist, Ph.D.

For ages 9–13. 128 pp.; PB; two-color; illust.; 5⅜" x 8⅜".

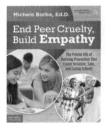

End Peer Cruelty, Build Empathy
The Proven 6Rs of Bullying Prevention That Create Inclusive, Safe, and Caring Schools
by Michele Borba, Ed.D.

For administrators, teachers, counselors, youth leaders, bullying prevention teams, and parents of children in grades K–8. 288 pp; PB; 7¼" x 9¼"; includes digital content.

Free PLC/Book Study Guide
freespirit.com/PLC

Interested in purchasing multiple quantities and receiving volume discounts?
Contact edsales@freespirit.com or call 1.800.735.7323 and ask for Education Sales.

Many Free Spirit authors are available for speaking engagements, workshops, and keynotes.
Contact speakers@freespirit.com or call 1.800.735.7323.

For pricing information, to place an order, or to request a free catalog, contact:

Free Spirit Publishing Inc. • 6325 Sandburg Road, Suite 100 • Minneapolis, MN 55427-3674
toll-free 800.735.7323 • local 612.338.2068 • fax 612.337.5050
help4kids@freespirit.com • www.freespirit.com